World's Best
Wildlife Dive Sites

NICK ROBERTSON-BROWN FRPS
AND CAROLINE ROBERTSON-BROWN MSc

First published in 2016 by Reed New Holland Publishers Pty Ltd
London • Sydney • Auckland

The Chandlery, Unit 704, 50 Westminster Bridge Road, London SE1 7QY, UK
1/66 Gibbes Street, Chatswood, NSW 2067, Australia
5/39 Woodside Avenue, Northcote, Auckland 0627, New Zealand

www.newhollandpublishers.com

A record of this book is held at the British Library and the National Library of Australia.

ISBN 978 1 92151 772 3

Managing Director: Fiona Schultz
Publisher and Project Editor: Simon Papps
Designer: Thomas Casey
Cover Design: Andrew Davies
Production Director: James Mills-Hicks
Printer: Toppan Leefung Printing Limited

1 3 5 7 9 10 8 6 4 2

Keep up with New Holland Publishers on Facebook
www.facebook.com/NewHollandPublishers

World's Best
Wildlife Dive Sites

NICK ROBERTSON-BROWN FRPS
AND CAROLINE ROBERTSON-BROWN MSC

Contents

Foreword

If diving, underwater photography, travel, adventure or all of the above lights your fire, at some stage you might be lucky enough to meet Nick and Caroline Robertson-Brown. If that fortune evades you, the next best way to benefit from their unrestrained enthusiasm for our underwater world, and their experience of it, would be to read this book. It's a diver's wish-list for exactly where to go in the world for the kind of excitement that ranges from the adrenaline-fuelled rush caused by big animals interacting in huge underwater scenes like the Sardine Run, to the sheer fascination for the sometimes bizarre creatures that live in the micro habitats of Bali.

We all know that more than two-thirds of our blue planet is covered in water, but this poses a problem. There is simply too much to explore. Despite my very best efforts, I know that I will never see everything that I want to see underwater. But this is where the book will help. It gives you the focus that we sometimes lack and the vicarious experience that you can take or leave according to personal taste. It helps you to narrow down where you might spend what is left of that most precious resource, which is of course your time.

Follow Nick and Caroline as they tour their favourite dive sites around the world. Seek inspiration from their words and beautiful images that will help you to launch your next big diving adventure. They really have been around the diving block, so to speak, so their advice is based on practical first-hand experience. I found it apposite and concise. It helps you to make the absolute most out of the limited time that we all have when we commit to new destinations. Despite the frequent assertion that we never have enough time, we are all allotted about the same in life and it ticks by at precisely the same rate for every one of us. It's how you use your time that matters. This book will help you and I commend you to make a modest investment by setting aside time to read it. It will help you squeeze so much more out of your next quest.

PAUL COLLEY

Paul Colley CB OBE is an underwater photographer and freelance journalist. Author of the acclaimed book Winning Images with Any Underwater Camera, *he won the British Wildlife Photography Awards (Coast and Marine) in 2015. He is a specialist in remote control photography for freshwater rivers and works with conservation groups including the Shark Trust, the Blue Marine Foundation and Fauna and Flora International, with whose people he is trying to make more images count in the conservation of our rivers and oceans.*

OPPOSITE *A diver with the dolphin statue that welcomes visitors to the caves at the Medes Islands.*

Introduction

When we were first asked to write this book, we carefully studied our portfolio to see which of the dive sites we had already recorded and then looked at what we needed in order to be able to create a definitive guide to our favourite dive sites around the world. We also needed to make sure that we could fulfil the criteria outlined to us by the publishers. As photojournalists for dive magazines and the national press, as well as having run dive shops at home in Manchester and in the Caribbean, we had a lot of experience in scouring the globe for underwater wildlife. Our media company, Frogfish Photography has been running for over 10 years and in that time we have accumulated over 5TB (5 terabytes) worth of high-resolution images. We were given 12 months to complete the task, and while we knew that it would be a challenge, which it was, we hadn't quite realised just how much work we had set ourselves. We are not asking for sympathy, it is a job that thousands of people would love to be offered and we did, of course, have a fabulous time trying to accumulate all the images and stories you can see in the 32 chapters within this book. The title of the book is emotive in itself and I can guarantee that there will be chapters which readers will challenge as being worthy of inclusion, however, choosing the *World's Best Wildlife Dive Sites* is, by its very nature, a subjective decision. In order to mitigate this, we have provided a fact panel in which we have included alternative dive sites for the key species that we have focused on.

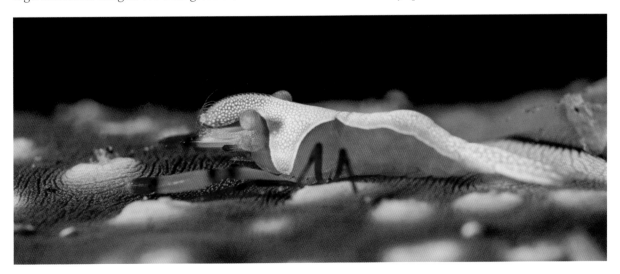

ABOVE *In the Lembeh Strait Emperor Shrimps ride on the back of sea cucumbers in a symbiotic relationship where they clean off parasites in return for a free ride and extra food.*

OPPOSITE *The pigs of Big Major Cay in the Exumas are surprisingly strong swimmers and will come right up to people who get in the water.*

Having made the decision on which dive sites and creatures we wanted to include in the publication, we set about organizing the travel and the logistics to collect the images. As every diver knows, however, you can arrive at your chosen dive location and even if you have a week to get all the images you need, Mother Nature hasn't necessarily read the script. There are some dive sites, for example, where we ended up only having one dive to get the images and fortunately it worked. The hammerheads of Bimini were a prime example of this, as it had been stormy for the previous two days, stirring up the water and sand and we really did have just the one chance to get what we wanted. In contrast, we spent a week on the Neptune Islands with Andrew Fox, only to coincide with the worst weather that they have had in South Australia for some time. As a result, while we got some lovely images of Great White Sharks in the distance, only very few of these would be suitable for this publication. Fortunately for us, Andrew is an excellent photographer and he donated several of his Great White images for this chapter.

We had problems in the Maldives where, despite following the pelagic route, we encountered the mantas on only two occasions – once on a night dive and once very fleetingly at the surface. A friend of ours and former student of mine, Sean Chinn, had far more luck than we did and several of the images in the manta chapter were, very kindly, donated by Sean. A lack of

LEFT *The Bohar Snapper at Ras Mohammed all move as one, as each individual has the ability to sense the fish in front turning and follow each movement exactly.*

OPPOSITE *The corals that live around the Turks and Caicos Islands often have beautiful sea snails living on them.*

ABOVE *Amongst the seaweed it has adapted to mimic, the Leafy Seadragon is nearly impossible to see, however they do stray away occasionally.*
OPPOSITE *Sometimes, due to reduced visibility, you cannot see the huge Basking Sharks until they are very close to you.*

time meant that a new acquaintance, Alex Misiewicz, kindly helped us out with images from New Zealand and 'Tourism and Event Queensland' provided images of the SS *Yongala* wreck. We had two opportunities for trips to see Whale Sharks, but both of these fell through and another friend, Daniel Norwood, gave us the superb images of these iconic creatures that you can see in the Mexico chapter. Finally, our trip to the Azores to capture the devil rays fell through but we were rescued by two good friends, Dave and Liz Skinner. We are very grateful to them all.

One of the most difficult judgements we had to make was regarding which were the 'best' 32 wildlife dive sites that should be included. Again it was a

totally subjective decision. As we only had limited time available, some of the decisions were obvious since we had already visited what we considered to be 20 of the best dive sites from the bucket-list that we produced for ourselves some 10 years ago. It was the final dozen sites that caused the most soul-searching and we came up with a list of 25 locations for potential inclusion. There are bound be readers screaming at the book and denouncing us for not including their own favourite places. We will continue with our quest to find another selection of dive sites and perhaps there will be a second volume of this book to follow in the future. In the meantime we hope that you enjoy our presentation of the 32 wildlife dive sites that we have selected here.

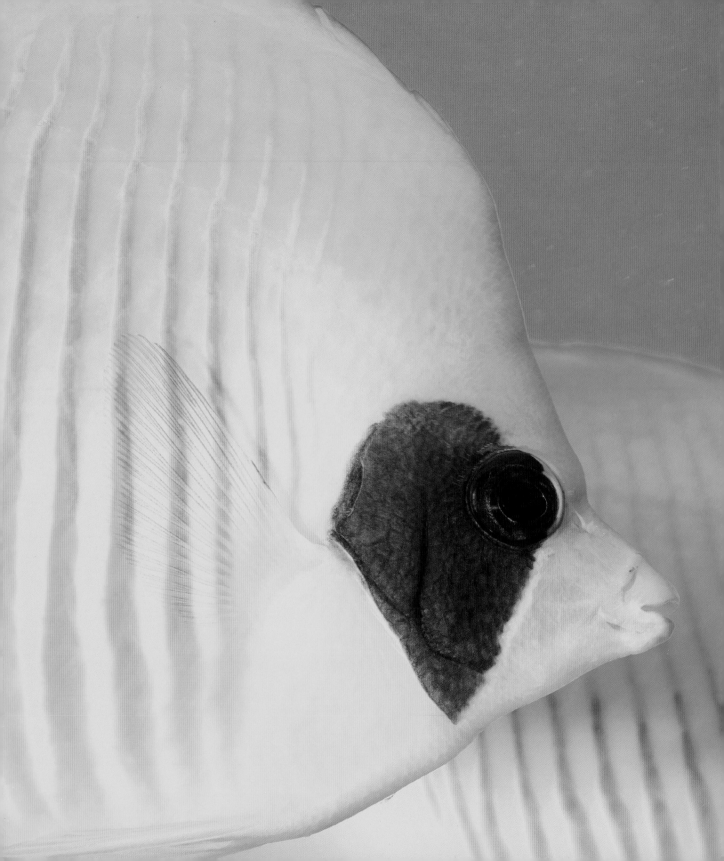

AFRICA

The Sardine Run

"The greatest shoal on Earth" – DAVID ATTENBOROUGH

The Sardine Run off the South African coastline is one of nature's truly great events. This phenomenon happens most years, although it does not occur every year and the reasons for this are not totally understood. It is believed by most scientists and observers that the sardines spawn off the southern tip of South Africa, several hundred miles out in the Agulhas Banks.

Usually between the months of May and June, the currents around this area become complicated, but when a cool current runs north from the southern tip of South Africa, close to the shore line, the sardines follow this in their millions. This enormous migration will take the sardines over 30 days to reach the east coast of KwaZulu-Natal. Once they have arrived here, the predators start to take notice and the fate of the South African Sardines or Pilchards (*Sardinops ocellatus*) is sealed.

Once this event has started, everything and everyone wants a piece of the action. Hundreds of fishermen chase the shoals as they head up north towards Durban. However, the real action, a drama-tragedy, plays itself out beneath the waves, and if you are lucky enough to be there you will be treated to an audio-visual feast of predator-prey interaction with numerous predators helping themselves to the individuals swarming in the silver band of sardines. These shoals can be enormous and they can stretch for something like 7–15km (4.5–9 miles) along the coast.

A huge variety of underwater predators follow the shoal, both above and below the water, with Bronze Whaler (*Carcharhinus brachyurus*), Dusky (*C. obscurus*) and Blacktip (*C. limbatus*) Sharks as well as various large game fish. Cape Fur Seals (*Arctocephalus pusillus*), Humpback (*Megaptera novaeangliae*), Southern Minke (*Balaenoptera bonaerensis*) and Bryde's (*B. brydei*) Whales all try and help themselves to a piece of the action. However, it is the dolphins that bring order

OPPOSITE *The action happens very quickly and before long all the fish are eaten and the show moves on.*

ABOVE *The boat launches can be very tricky as the coastline here is rugged and the waves very large.*

OPPOSITE *Humpback Whales migrate up the South African coast at the same time as the Sardine Run.*

to this mayhem. The pods primarily consist of Long-beaked Common Dolphin. However, pods of bottlenose dolphins (genus *Tursiops*) have been known to find their way to this event. Working in massive pods, sometimes so large that they are known as super-pods, and communicating with each other all the time, these beautiful, elegant and incredibly intelligent creatures break up the shoals into large, but manageable numbers. Once they have separated a large group of sardines, they encircle it, somewhat like a 'wild west' scene of Native Americans attacking a wagon train! They release bubbles from their blowholes and make high-pitched noises as they talk to the rest of the pod. This contains the sardines using a curtain of air-bubbles, which expand on their way to the surface. As the bubbles increase in size, the pod members slowly and patiently circle and bring this bait ball to the surface. Up until this point, the noise underwater has been incredible as the dolphins

screech and whistle as they communicate with each other. But then, suddenly, it all goes quiet, deathly quiet, but only for a few seconds. The sardines seem to sense that this is the moment they have all been dreading and the silver ball starts to flash wildly as the sardines take up their protean defence. Once again, the cacophony of noise starts up, but this time it is even louder as the gannets, cormorants and terns hit the surface with a loud crash, diving in to try and grab a meal. The noise the gannets make as they hit the surface sounds like muffled gunfire. The dolphins shoot left and right and yet appear to have some semblance of order as to which individuals of their pod are allowed to go in first, but they all seem to get a fair share. Meanwhile, lower down, the sharks that had been circling at the bottom of the ball, in huge numbers, start to join in the feeding frenzy, apparently acknowledging the seniority of the dolphins who have marshalled and conjured the whole event.

ABOVE TOP *During quieter moments you can take in the huge numbers of whales, dolphins, sharks and birds from the boat.*

ABOVE BOTTOM *The Common Dolphins burst through the bait ball grabbing the fish as they go.*

OPPOSITE TOP *Common Dolphins round up the sardines into tight balls for the whole pod to feast on.*

OPPOSITE BOTTOM *Sharks stay deeper than the dolphins, pushing the bait ball nearer the surface.*

Depending on the size of the shoal, the whole performance rarely lasts for more than about 10 to 15 minutes, and by the end of it, not a single individual sardine survives. During one such event, I observed a solitary sardine, totally confused and bemused, not knowing what to do or where to go. In an instant, a Common Dolphin shot across my field of view and the unfortunate sardine was gone; what was once a seething mass of predator-prey interaction was now a quiet, empty sea, full of glistening scales, slowly sinking to the sea floor.

The Sardine Run is a magnificent event, but many hours are spent patrolling at the surface, looking for the signs that can give away what is happening beneath the waves. It is much easier to spot an event if the sea is calm and sometimes it is just too rough to even venture out. Indeed, the waves that break along the south-east tip of this magnificent country are infamous. The boat launch is one of the most exciting events of the day, whether you find a bait ball or not. The guys that drive the large RIBs have to negotiate several lines of incoming waves and escape out to beyond the waves that break along the seashore. This negotiation calls for skill and patience on the part of the boat captain and as a passenger you would need to make sure you have your feet in the foot pockets and your hands firmly gripping the handles or line along the side of the RIB. Once you have made it out into the open sea, the day begins and you can start to scan the surface for any signs of sardine action. Usually, the best indicators are the gannets falling from the sky like dive-bombers to penetrate the surface of the sea. Some operators will follow the pods of dolphins, but the best, generally, work in small teams and use radio to call between themselves if any

Port St Johns
SOUTH AFRICA

KEY SPECIES
Long-beaked Common Dolphin (*Delphinus capensis*).

BEST TIME TO VISIT
The Sardine Run in South Africa can occur any time from May to July.

TIPS FOR VISITORS
This can be an adrenalin-filled trip and you need to be fit enough to get in and out of a large RIB multiple times in the day to get the most out of it. You may also want to consider brushing up on your freediving skills, as there are times when putting on your scuba gear is simply not an option. Stay for as long as you can, so that you increase your chance of being there for the peak of the action.

EQUIPMENT TO TAKE
The waters in South Africa at this time of year are cool and you will need a thick wetsuit, hood and gloves. Ensure you have both an underwater camera and a separate one for shots taken from the boat, in order that you can record all the amazing encounters.

ALTERNATIVE TOP DIVE SITES
There are other impressive aggregations of sardines, with the most attention going to Moalboal in the Philippines, but nothing beats a good year at the South African Sardine Run.

signs of bait-balling are apparent. Others may have a pilot in a microlight scanning the surface of the sea for any tell-tale signs, although planes, helicopters and microlights tend to be expensive and are mostly used by television companies and film crews. Many operators choose to use these hours on the surface to get close to some of the hundreds of Humpback Whales heading north on their migration along the same coast that the sardines use. This can offer a great opportunity to attempt to photograph these whales up close and personal, both at the surface and beneath the waves. With luck, you may see Bryde's Whales or Southern Minke Whales, but you will be really unlucky not to have close encounters with Humpbacks. When a Humpback arrives it is a magical moment. If this marine Leviathan is in the right frame of mind, then he or she may follow the boat alongside and just below the surface. In playful mood they can breach, lifting their body, which can weigh up to 17 tons, almost entirely clear of the water to fall back to the surface with a resounding crash. Pectoral fin slapping is another of their idiosyncrasies and it is believed that both of these actions are at least partially used by the whale to try and shake off some of the numerous parasites that attach themselves to the surface of their bodies. However, one of the most beautiful, and photographed, moments is when they slip serenely beneath the surface and their tail fluke rises and falls in sinusoidal motion, trailing water as it disappears. This is, of course, likely to trigger mixed emotions; has this beautiful giant left you, or will it return in a few minutes time?

BELOW *Whilst waiting for the main event, dolphins socialize and can be photographed whilst diving.*

Diving with the Blacktip Sharks of Aliwal Shoal

Lying on the South African coast, a short distance south of Durban is a small town called Rocky Bay. Several miles off the coastline, the currents well up to bring nutrients to the surface and it is here that the large, pelagic Blacktip Sharks have arrived and adapted their behaviour over the past few years.

By their nature, sharks of this species are normally solitary animals that do not shoal, but in this relatively small area, large numbers of them have aggregated into a pack of hunters. Not only is this behaviour unusual, but it appears that every member of this shoal is female and there is a definite social structure amongst them with one large female who is clearly the Alpha. If you get the chance to be in the water with this particular shoal you can observe for yourself how all the other sharks give way to this one senior female.

It is not entirely understood what has caused this behavioural change, but it is more than possible that the regular chumming of the waters to bring in the sharks for photojournalism may have contributed to what is happening. It is not just the divers with their cameras, however, as there are many fishing boats that are chartered by game fishermen and this has encouraged the sharks to follow the boats and grab the catch from the lines. There may be some other factors that have affected this behaviour, but the wily females seem to have learned and adapted to the 'free lunch' principle with great success.

Whatever the reasons for this unusual behaviour it makes for spectacular diving, with sometimes up to 60 of these magnificent predators circling and following the chum as the whole set-up drifts along with the prevailing current. When the conditions are right the Blacktip Sharks may be joined by Tiger Sharks (*Galeocerdo cuvier*) and even Bull Sharks (*Carcharhinus leucas*) turning up to grab a piece of the action.

OPPOSITE *Two Blacktip Sharks come in close to the divers.*

24

ABOVE *South Africa offers a great chance to get out on safari.*
OPPOSITE *This group of Blacktip Sharks are all females. They gather in large numbers when attracted by chum.*

If you have never dived in South Africa before, then your first experiences will be amazing. The first exciting experience that you will encounter is the launch. The large RIBs that all operators use here are launched from the beach by using a tractor with a long pole on the end which pushes you out into the surf. The big waves are just a little further out and are regularly 4–5m (13–16ft) high. The RIB captains here really earn their crusts as one wrong move can very easily lead to the RIB being flipped. The boats have straps on the floor which are designed for you to put your feet into, and in addition you hang on to the handles and stringers along the side of the RIB with both hands. Once you have passed the surf line the sea usually calms down. However, to get past the surf involves several somewhat exciting moments as the captain looks for any gaps, or gates, in the surf lines. When he sees a gap, the powerful twin motors on the back of the RIB are gunned and you head for that gap at full speed. The captain will have already seen and chosen the gate on the next wave heading towards the shore and if that closes up he will immediately turn the boat around and head in the direction of the shore, very quickly. These guys are really good and the chance of a mishap occurring is slim, but should you choose to go to South Africa to dive off the south-east coast then make sure that you are comfortable with the operator you have chosen.

ABOVE *A diver reaches out to a shark during a bait experience. The shark has clearly been injured by a fisherman recently.*

Once you have cleared the surf lines the sea generally calms down and it is a relatively flat ride as the RIB hydroplanes across the waves. All the same, this experience is not for the fainthearted! It is fast and furious and you are hanging on with your feet in the stirrups for some time before you reach a suitable site on the Aliwal Shoal.

Once you arrive at the site, the first thing that will happen is that the boat is anchored and the chum, which is broken-up sardine or mackerel, is thrown into the water. Because the boat is anchored up, the current carries a fish oil-slick along the surface and

within a few minutes the slick is over 100m (330ft) long. It seems like an age before anything else happens, but usually within 40 minutes or so you will see those familiar bronze dorsal fins creating a wake as they cruise around the RIB, seeking the source of the fish oil. At this point it is time to start donning your scuba gear, but you will not be entering the water just yet. Most operators use a washing machine drum filled with sardines which is attached to a large buoy with a 10m (33ft) line. This is thrown over the side, attached to a line on the anchor line, and then it is time to sit back and wait a little longer. The anchor is raised and the RIB drifts along with the current, surrounded by

ABOVE *At first you have to overcome any fear and just get in the water.*

the fish-oil slick. When there are sufficient sharks surrounding the boat you will be allowed to enter the water, and if you've not done it before then this really is a leap of faith, but it is one that is absolutely worth it. You need to use a negative entry technique so that you can immediately drop down to be looking up at the circling sharks. If you have a camera and you are there to take images, then all you have to do is wait for these wonderful predators to approach. As the bait drum is hanging off the back of the boat and the boat is drifting, the whole set-up drifts along with the current and there is no need to fin against this current. You all move along something like a hot-

air balloon, except that it all takes place underwater. Most operators use a diver or a free diver to pull the sardines from the drum, and at the same time the captain or one of the crew will steadily throw sardines into the water to help keep the sharks interested.

If you have a camera and want to try and get some shots, then the best course of action is to try and line yourself up with an individual shark that is heading towards you. They do seem to be attracted to the sound of recharging strobes and these can help you get the best shot. They may even try to grab the strobe, so be aware and

Aliwal Shoal
SOUTH AFRICA

KEY SPECIES
Blacktip Shark (*Carcharhinus limbatus*).

BEST TIME TO VISIT
You can shark-dive at Aliwal Shoal all year round, but conditions, water temperatures and species of shark will all vary depending on what season you choose. The water is calmest from March to August.

TIPS FOR VISITORS
Make sure that you are happy with the dive operator you select. Diving with sharks is a serious business and it is best to do this with a seasoned professional who puts safety before profit. The boat launches here are exhilarating and you need to be confident diving from a RIB (Rigid Inflatable Boat) and be strong enough to hang on during rough entries and exits.

EQUIPMENT TO TAKE
The water can be cool, and you will want to stay in the water for as long as possible, so take a warm wetsuit, hood and gloves. Make sure that all of your equipment is black, or predominantly dark, as most operators will insist that you do not wear brightly coloured neoprene masks or fins.

ALTERNATIVE TOP DIVE SITES
This is the only place that you can realistically dive with a large group of this species of shark with confidence.

ready! If you are not using strobes, then you must remember to set your shutter speed to at least 1/250th of a second to avoid any motion blur.

If you decide to go to South Africa to dive Aliwal Shoal, bear in mind that there are many other great underwater photography experiences within a radius of a few hundred miles. Just a short distance away is a great dive and photo opportunity at Proteus Banks. Here you can see Ragged-tooth Sharks (*Carcharias taurus*), which appear to smile at you as they swim past. It also has a host of other experiences, including Great White Shark (*Carcharodon carcharias*) cage-diving and the opportunity of seeing Killer Whales (*Orcinus orca*) near Cape Town, where there are also huge seal colonies.

In summary, South Africa is a fabulous place for the underwater photography trip of a lifetime. However, I strongly advise that you select a reputable tour company with experienced and knowledgeable guides. Get recommendations from people you know who have been there, and this will help to give you the peace of mind that goes with venturing on an exciting yet expensive trip. Above all, get fit! All the boat diving is from RIBs, with challenging surf launches and big seas. If you are lucky then your boat rides to the dive sites will be interrupted by snorkelling with whales, dolphins, manta rays and Whale Sharks (*Rhincodon typus*) which, combined with underwater photography, can become very tiring. Also, get some time in at your local swimming pool to try and improve your freediving skills. This will help you to get the most from your large animal encounters. Diving in South Africa with the right people in the right places is an unsurpassable experience for divers and underwater photographers alike.

ABOVE TOP *Three Blacktip Sharks avoid a collision as they circle the boat.*

ABOVE MIDDLE *This can be an adrenalin-filled experience as the sharks will come in very close.*

ABOVE BOTTOM *The Blacktip Shark is an impressive sight close up and you can expect plenty of opportunitiy to see and photograph them on this dive.*

Gatherings of Bohar Snapper
at Ras Mohammed

For divers who live in Europe, probably the easiest place to get
to for some first-class, warm-water diving and great biodiversity
has to be Egypt and the Red Sea. The water temperature never
drops below 19°C (66°F), and that is the exception. The lowest
temperatures are usually 20–21°C (68–70°F) and it is over
25°C (77°F) for most of the year.

A week's diving, either on a liveaboard or land-based, is not expensive and there are numerous dive sites offering a range of types of diving. Many of the best dive sites are very rarely used as the operators feel the urge to take their divers to the famous ones, and keeping to known locations also helps them to stay on schedule. There are some particularly popular times for divers to go to the Red Sea to indulge their passion, but a lot of this timing is dependent upon what you want to see. Throughout the winter months the weather can be a little bit unpredictable, with high winds that can make the sailing somewhat uncomfortable, but it is unusual not to be able to dive at all. In many ways July is the best time to go, but it is a very popular time and hence can be crowded. July and August can also be extremely hot, and those from colder climates may find themselves struggling with the heat when not in the water. The principal reason that July has become so popular with people who want to see wildlife, rather than the wrecks, is due to a basic biological need – sex. This is the time of the year when many of the fish and the other creatures in the sea are looking to procreate, and for divers, and particularly photographers, the opportunities are at their most prolific.

One of the greatest spectacles that you can witness in the Red Sea, in July, is the aggregation of the Bohar Snapper, which belongs to the family Lutjanidae. When fish group together it is usually for a reason, but the gathering is not always structured. Sometimes an aggregation of fish can be a totally mixed group of species that is searching for food.

OPPOSITE *Bohar Snapper are a lovely looking fish and seem to vary in colour depending on how much light catches their scales.*

When they come together and interact socially, the dynamic changes and this interaction is referred to as 'shoaling', but shoaling can still refer to a loose group where individuals may forage independently or break off into smaller groups. It is when the shoal takes on some order and becomes more organised, with the fish moving together at the same speed and in the same direction, that they can be said to be schooling. Schooling fish can present an amazing display as they tend to synchronise their movements and adopt a protean defence in the face of predators. This defensive system is common in nature. It is a system that sees the fish move and change direction together, maintaining the same distance between each other, and this causes the light to reflect off their scales simultaneously to create confusion to any predator trying to select an individual as its prey. A genuine school of fish is usually all of the same species, with individuals being of similar size and age, although very often there can be the odd individual of another species which has inserted itself into the school as protection for itself.

The Bohar Snapper can grow to a length in excess of 85cm (33in), although most individuals do not exceed 75cm (30in). They are mainly reddish-brown, but their fins appear to be a much darker, plainer brown. Interestingly, during the schooling period in July, when they aggregate for spawning purposes, they appear to be more red than brown. It is a particularly long-lived species which matures at around eight to nine years and can live to over 50 years of age; one individual is known to have lived to the age of 56. It is unfortunate that overfishing, particularly with the use of modern, high-tech fishing methods, means very few individuals will make it to this ripe old age.

ABOVE *The schools of snapper can be very large, perhaps a similar size to the boat that you arrive to the dive site on.*

OPPOSITE *Divers must approach the school with caution so as not to split the fish and cause them stress.*

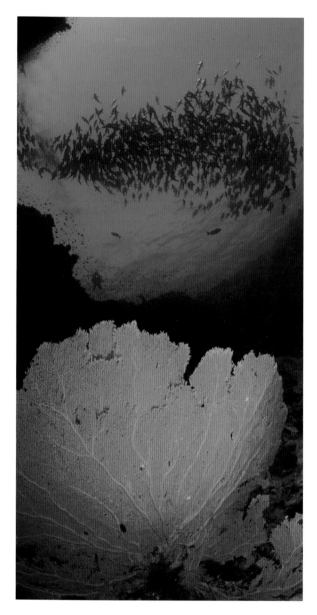

ABOVE *Whilst getting in and around the school is ideal, they are also beautiful to photograph from below with the reef.*

OPPOSITE *The schools can form twirling shapes that look like a fish tornado.*

The species is sometimes referred to by its alternative common names of Red Bass, Twinspot Snapper or Two-spot Red Snapper. The last two names are derived from the fact that the juveniles have two white spots on their back, adjacent to their dorsal fins. These two spots disappear or may become red as the fish matures.

The Bohar Snapper is viewed as an intelligent fish and one example of this is that immatures are well-known to use mimicry to help them catch prey. They mimic the behaviour of non-predatory damselfish and once they get close enough to their prey, they attack and eat it.

For most of the year this large species of snapper can be found on coral reefs alone as it searches for prey. Once a year, however, they aggregate into huge schools which can number several hundred individuals swimming in circles and forming a conical spiral that can twist and turn and swoop over the reef like a single, enormous entity.

Being in the water and watching one of these huge schools spiralling in front of you is truly spellbinding. Often they will hang out at around 30m (100ft) or more from the edge of a reef with nothing but blue water completely around and below this gently moving mass of red fish that looks silver-blue until illuminated with artificial light. This enormous ball, however, can be very easily broken up by careless or ignorant divers rushing into the middle in an effort to be a part of it. I have been with a group of disciplined divers and photographers who had been moving slowly and gently around the school using their exhaled bubbles, like dolphins on the Sardine Run, to compress the school in a tighter and tighter cone. Unfortunately, if there are any other dive

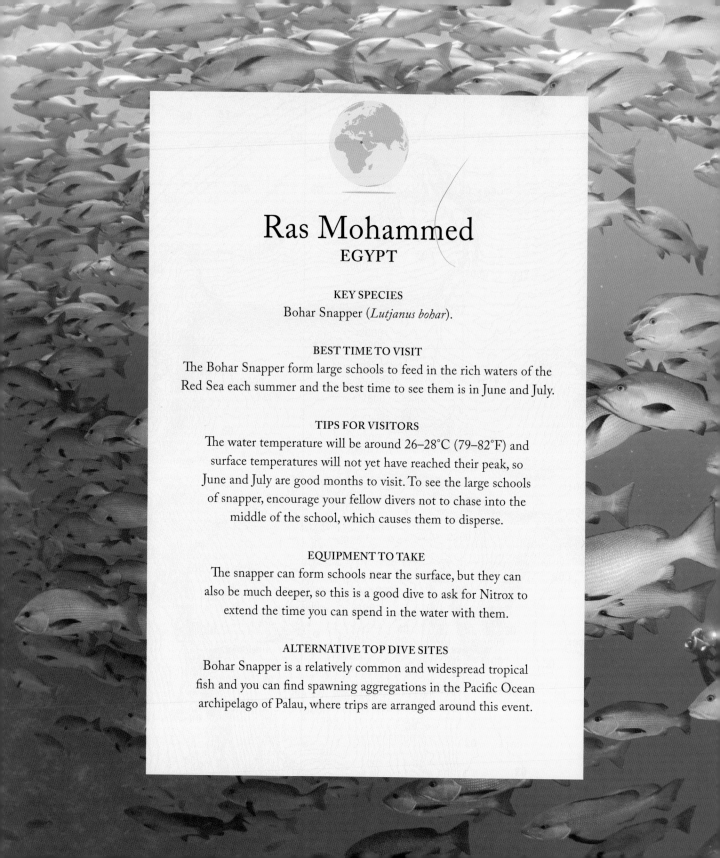

Ras Mohammed
EGYPT

KEY SPECIES
Bohar Snapper (*Lutjanus bohar*).

BEST TIME TO VISIT
The Bohar Snapper form large schools to feed in the rich waters of the Red Sea each summer and the best time to see them is in June and July.

TIPS FOR VISITORS
The water temperature will be around 26–28°C (79–82°F) and surface temperatures will not yet have reached their peak, so June and July are good months to visit. To see the large schools of snapper, encourage your fellow divers not to chase into the middle of the school, which causes them to disperse.

EQUIPMENT TO TAKE
The snapper can form schools near the surface, but they can also be much deeper, so this is a good dive to ask for Nitrox to extend the time you can spend in the water with them.

ALTERNATIVE TOP DIVE SITES
Bohar Snapper is a relatively common and widespread tropical fish and you can find spawning aggregations in the Pacific Ocean archipelago of Palau, where trips are arranged around this event.

ABOVE *These large schools of snapper are common in the summer months of June and July off Ras Mohammed.*

boats around, you may find that they do not share your discipline and I know from bitter experience that it takes only one enthusiastic and probably inexperienced diver to undo all your hard work.

This amazing event happens every year at the ubiquitously-named Shark Reef, which is inside the famous Ras Mohammed National Park in the northern part of the Red Sea. This whole area of the Red Sea can become very crowded during the months of June and July, as it is really popular with divers. There are numerous dive sites in this region, and not far away is another particularly good site called Yolanda Reef, which is close enough to be enjoyed on the same day. There are so many great dive sites in the Ras Mohammed National Park that many liveaboard dive operators offer a whole week's diving in this area alone.

The Reef Fish of Canyon

If you head north for 80km (50 miles) from Sharm el-Sheikh, which lies at the southern end of the Sinai Peninsula, you will arrive at a town called Dahab, which was once a small Bedouin fishing village. The name Dahab literally means 'gold' in Arabic, which is possibly a reference to the fact that gold was washed down from the mountains that overlook this small town and may have accumulated on the floodplain where the original village was built. Other suggestions are that it's a reference to the colour of the sand or the sky just after sunset.

The town of Dahab was once three separate villages lying in close proximity along the west coast of the Gulf of Aqaba. In the north is the original Bedouin village of Asalah; a little further south is Mashraba, where most of the tourist hotels are now located; and further south is Medina, which has become famous for windsurfing. Dahab became known to Westerners in the 1960s when backpackers sought solitude and relaxation at the remote camps and hostels.

The atmosphere in the town of Dahab still has that laid-back hippie feel that made it such a favourite hideaway in the 1960s and 1970s. The diving also has an easy-going feel to it as all the dives are from the shore and, even if you wish to indulge in three dives

in the day, or even four if you take in a night-dive, it never feels rushed and some of the night-dives here are spectacular. Dahab is also an ideal place for the novice diver and photographer as currents are rarely an issue and great visibility is a given. The most famous site in Dahab is probably the Blue Hole which, sadly, has a reputation for being the world's most dangerous dive-site. This is an unkind tag, as it is not the dive site that is dangerous, but the technical and non-technical divers who want to break the rules. The bottom of the dive site is at a depth of 100m (330ft), but there is an arch in the hole at around 54m (177ft), which too many recreational divers cannot resist the challenge of diving through. Once these divers have reached the entrance of the arch it is a further 35m (115ft) of finning before they

OPPOSITE *A clownfish displays to the photographer whilst defending its anemone.*

ABOVE *Humphead Wrasse are one of the largest fish you will see in Dahab and they are happy to approach divers.*
OPPOSITE *There is a wonderful coral reef wall in Dahab that attracts turtles to feed on the sponges that squeeze between the corals.*

can begin their ascent. Many young men have died, but only through sheer stupidity and arrogance and it is a shame that the Blue Hole is now infamous as a result of dangerous challenges and dares.

My favourite dive site at this Sinai resort, however, is Canyon. It gets its name from a 20m (65ft) long fissure in the seabed at a depth of around 14m (46ft). The canyon itself drops down to 30m (98ft), but you can exit that gap at 18m (60ft), which takes you out from the wall and into the blue water of the gulf. The site is accessed from the shore via a shallow lagoon, with a saddle (a gap in the reef) which you pass through, and this then takes you gently downwards over a sandy coral garden towards the entrance to the Canyon. The opening to the Canyon is not very wide, but there is sufficient space to allow a free descent as the cavern widens until you reach the bottom. Sunlight penetrates the cavern, providing not only sufficient light for you to see the numerous glassfish swirling in the corner, but also to create stunning photographic opportunities using the shards of light that bounce in front of you. Once you have exited the Canyon you can turn back on yourself and swim over the surrounding seabed, which is porous and this allows you to swim through your own bubbles as you head back through the coral garden.

Returning through the coral garden is relaxing and as you check the no-decompression-limit (NDL)

ABOVE *Anthias are the tiny fish that dart in and out of their coral homes as you breathe and your bubbles scare them into hiding.*

OPPOSITE TOP *Pufferfish take a rest by balancing on the coral tops at night.*

OPPOSITE BOTTOM *Hawkfish hide among the corals and dart off at the slightest disturbance.*

on your computer, you should see that there is now plenty of time to meander back to the entrance of the lagoon as most of it is between 10–5m (33–16.5ft). The floor is littered with anemones, all hosting their guardians, the Two-banded Clownfish, which are also known as Two-banded Anemonefish. It is often said by divers that if clownfish were much bigger than they are, then diving anywhere near them would be dangerous. I've seen numerous divers come back from a dive sporting bite wounds from the large female anemonefish guarding her host and her young. It is usually the female that bites the inquisitive diver as there is a strict hierarchy and the largest and most aggressive of the group is a female. She wasn't always a female, however, as clownfish are hermaphrodites and start their lives as males. It is only once they mature that they may become female and there is only one male and one female in the group that will reproduce. Clownfish form symbiotic relationships with their anemones, each providing one another with protection (called mutualism). The stinging cells in the tentacles of the anemone will deter predators from taking the clownfish, which itself is immune to the sting of the anemone. There can be colour variations from population to population in this species of clownfish, but all the individuals tend to be similar in the same area. The clownfish of Dahab are all bright orange.

Another really common, but fascinating, species that you can expect to see is the lionfish, which seems to be carving a niche for itself almost anywhere in the world where the water is warm. This is partly due to the fact that the female lionfish regularly produces up to 15,000 eggs, and also that they have very few natural predators. There are several species of lionfish, but the Clearfin Lionfish (*Pterois*

ABOVE *A diver swims through the bubbles created by the divers in the canyon below.*

OPPOSITE *A lionfish hovers upside-down at the entrance to the canyon.*

radiata) and Common Lionfish (*Pterois miles*) are the two most common species that you will see at Dahab. It is easy to distinguish between the two as the larger Common Lionfish has broader spines on its fins, which are more brightly-coloured. Both species have feather-like fins and they are covered with reddish-brown and white stripes but, as most people are aware, caution is required as the pectoral fins are venomous and a sting from a lionfish is exceedingly painful and debilitating. Lionfish are not particularly aggressive to divers but you do need to show caution and be aware of where they are around you. This is particularly so on a night dive, as large numbers are prone to accumulate around your dive light in the hope that you may illuminate their dinner. Lionfish are insatiable predators which are quite happy to hunt on their own but have regularly been seen hunting in packs when they shepherd their prey into a small area to make their kills.

There are numerous fish and animal species, not just on the Canyon dive site, but also on any of the 20

Dahab
EGYPT

KEY SPECIES
Two-banded Clownfish (*Amphiprion bicinctus*).

BEST TIME TO VISIT
If you want warm water then the best time to visit is during the summer
months between June and October. It is possible to dive all year round
here, but in winter the water temperatures can drop to 21°C (70°F).

TIPS FOR VISITORS
This is a great destination for those who are new to diving, as there
is little current and the dive sites are mostly easy-going. Some dive
sites, such as the Blue Hole, can get very busy indeed, so it is best to
avoid the peak season of August and September (the school summer
holidays in Europe) if you want your dive a little less crowded.

EQUIPMENT TO TAKE
Wear boots on all the dives, as you often start and finish the dive walking
out over the sand and there is a chance you may stand on a small piece
of coral or other stinging marine life. A thin wetsuit is fine in the
summer months, but you will need to take a thicker one for the winter.

ALTERNATIVE TOP DIVE SITES
Clownfish of various different species can be found in
many tropical dive sites, but the waters around Indonesia
and the Red Sea are the best destinations.

dive sites or so along a 10km (6 miles) stretch of the shoreline of Dahab. Virtually any reef species found in the Red Sea can be found at Dahab and the fringing reefs that border the shoreline are rich in coral and sponge diversity. It has been suggested that much of the diversity here is as a result of there being no fresh water running onto the reef, and the water temperatures remaining relatively constant throughout the year.

Over the past few years, there has been damage to some of the dive sites as a result of tourism and the building of hotels and artificial extensions into the sea. Most of the dive sites, however, including Canyon, are still in good condition and Canyon on a night dive is truly spectacular.

BELOW *A juvenile lionfish takes shelter in the seagrass beds that line the shallower waters in Dahab.*

The Oceanic Whitetip Sharks
of the Brothers Islands

The excitement of diving at the Brothers starts even as you are
mooring up, usually the evening before you start your diving here.
As you peer over the rails of the boat, just as night falls, and the
boat's running lights cast a gloom in the water below, you will
see the Oceanic Whitetip Sharks cruising slowly around.

These sharks like to swim just below the surface, often very close to the boats, perhaps hoping for food scraps to be thrown over the side. The Brothers, locally known as El Akhawein, are made up of two islands situated over 65km (40 miles) off the mainland of Egypt. Boats usually depart from Port Ghalib, near Marsa Alam airport, and the journey can take around 5–7 hours depending on the weather conditions. Big Brother, the larger of the two, has a lighthouse which was built by the British in 1883 and is now maintained and used by the Egyptian military. Little Brother lies just one kilometre (0.6 miles) to the south. These islands lie right in the middle (width-ways) of the Red Sea and so are hugely influenced by weather and currents. The remote location of these islands, far out of sight

of any other landmass, makes diving here feel like an old-school shark-diving expedition, filling you with excitement and expectation as the time approaches when you will drop into the clear blue water.

Big Brother was formed by volcanic activity and the island that has formed is one of steep cliffs descending into the deep blue water. The strong currents bringing in nutrients, combined with steep walls descending to great depths, make this a popular site with many species of shark. Looking out into the blue you have a chance of spotting thresher sharks (genus *Alopias*), Scalloped Hammerhead Sharks (*Sphyrna lewini*), reef sharks, Silky Sharks (*Carcharhinus falciformis*) and, of course, the Oceanic Whitetip too.

OPPOSITE *An Oceanic Whitetip Shark turns away from the camera.*

As well as diving deeper to visit the many cleaning stations in the search for thresher sharks, and looking out into the blue for lone or schooling hammerheads, the dives here offer wonderful, healthy corals covering the walls. There are reef fish everywhere and you are certain to encounter turtles and Humphead Wrasse (*Cheilinus undulatus*) too.

The large liveaboard boats moor in the most sheltered part of the island and you will take RIBs (or zodiacs, as they are called here) to the dive sites further round each island. The determining factors on where you dive, and in what direction, will be the waves, wind and currents. Experienced boat captains and dive guides will assess the ever-changing conditions before each dive. If the weather allows, then there are also two excellent wrecks on Big Brother: the *Numidia* and the *Aida II*. Both structures lie with parts of the wreck in relatively shallow water, around 20m (65ft), but both also have structure that goes much deeper and so you need to watch your depth as you dive them.

To see the Oceanic Whitetips, the best plan is to dive in areas close to where the boat is moored, and allow for time on your return from a dive on the reef, or simply spend the whole dive under the moored-up dive boats. If you hang out at depths of around 5m (16ft), this will keep you away from the boat traffic and the regular propellers overhead. You do need to keep an eye on the surface at all times, as boat traffic can be busy and divers' bubbles can be difficult to spot in these sometimes hectic waters. Wait in one spot, just on the side of the boats that face out to sea, and if you are lucky an Oceanic Whitetip will come to see you. They are curious sharks and will come in close to divers, swimming past at a comfortable, unrushed pace

ABOVE TOP *Oceanic Whitetips tend to swim near the surface and are prone to boat strikes, especially on the dorsal fin.*

ABOVE MIDDLE *A shark checking out the photographer.*

ABOVE BOTTOM *Oceanic Whitetips circling.*

OPPOSITE *Pilot Fish can often be seen 'leading' the Oceanic Whitetip Sharks.*

Another Oceanic Whitetip with its posse of Pilot Fish in attendance.
An Oceanic Whitetip Shark in 'relaxed' mood with its large pectoral fins in normal position.

before disappearing off into the blue, soon returning for another swim-past. Look around deeper and you may also spot a Silky Shark coming closer for a look at you. The Silky Sharks here are more timid, though, and once spotted tend to head back to deeper water.

Oceanic Whitetip Sharks are very distinctive, with huge, rounded fins with a white patch at the end of each fin. This shark's Latin name, *longimanus*, means 'long hands', which describes superbly the pectoral fins of this beautiful shark. They have a worldwide distribution in waters with temperatures from 20–29 °C (68–84°F), and were once extremely common. Sadly, their numbers have now declined to worryingly low levels due to fishermen catching them for their

prized fins, which end up in soup in Asia. These sharks are often accompanied by black-and-white striped pilot fish, which swim alongside the shark in the hope of picking up scraps when the shark feeds, and are also known to remove parasites from the shark's skin.

Oceanic Whitetips swim at a leisurely pace, patrolling in shallow water for opportunistic meals. They will follow boats in the hope that, for example, fishing boats might discard some of their catch, or that diving boats will throw uneaten food overboard. It is quite possible that you will see the same individual shark at Little Brother that you have just dived with at Big Brother, as they can make the short journey across to the next island with you.

Brothers Islands
EGYPT

KEY SPECIES
Oceanic Whitetip Shark (*Carcharhinus longimanus*).

BEST TIME TO VISIT
The peak shark-watching period at these islands
is in October and November.

TIPS FOR VISITORS
Make sure that you get plenty of time to do an extended safety stop
under the boats, as this is where you are most likely to see the Oceanic
Whitetips in shallow water. Be prepared for deep dives in strong current
out into the blue. This is a dive site for more experienced divers.

EQUIPMENT TO TAKE
The water is still warm during October and November, at around
28–29°C (82–84°F), so a 3mm full wetsuit should be fine.

ALTERNATIVE TOP DIVE SITES
Cat Island in the Bahamas is another great destination to see these sharks.

ABOVE *Oceanic Whitetip circling the divers in the water.*

Many of the whitetips that you see at the Brothers will have injuries. As they swim so close to the surface, boat strikes are not uncommon and many of the sharks also have wounds from having been caught by people fishing and using a gaff to bring the shark on board. Some have hooks and fishing line still hanging out of their mouths. As they swim under the dives boats at the Brothers, they seem to get into a routine and follow a similar path around the boats, so after about half an hour in the water, you can work out which direction they will be coming from and position yourself to meet them. They appear to be attracted to anything shiny and will come in very close to investigate such items.

It is rare to get such a close encounter with a species of shark such as the Oceanic Whitetip without using bait and so seeing these sharks at the Brothers Islands is an extra special treat. If you time your trip well, and find a time when the sharks are present but the hordes of divers that come here in peak months have departed, you can have one of the finest shark experiences that diving has to offer. And the best thing about this is that it is all on the sharks' own terms. They come to see you because they 'want' to, and the spectacle is truly breathtaking.

EUROPE

The Basking Sharks of the West Coast of the United Kingdom

Many divers from Europe and the UK in particular, will travel thousands of miles in search of the Whale Shark. And yet, on the south-west and west coasts of the United Kingdom, an equally impressive encounter is available.

The Basking Sharks are one of the highlights of the UK underwater photography calendar, which begins in spring as plankton blooms and starts to draw these elusive creatures close in to these shores. The first sightings are usually off the battered and rugged coast of Cornwall, but as the spring turns to summer and even late autumn, the Basking Sharks continue their journey, swimming along the western coastline with sightings from locations as far apart as Land's End and John O'Groats. This plankton bloom, which attracts the world's second biggest fish, is caused by upwelling as a result of warmer water meeting the cooler inshore water off the coast. This brings nutrient-rich water, full of phytoplankton, to the surface where it photosynthesises. These microscopic plants are at the very base of the marine food chain and their existence leads to a huge increase in the numbers of zooplankton which feed upon these microscopic marine plants.

The zooplankton is what the Basking Sharks feed on and that is why they follow the plankton bloom along the southern and western coasts of the United Kingdom.

Despite their size, and the fact that they are so visible during the non-winter months, relatively little research has been done on the life history of the Basking Shark. It is the only member of the Cetorhinidae family of sharks and is known to be ovoviviparous, which means that the female produces eggs, but retains them until they have completely developed. They then hatch inside the female, who gives birth to fully-developed young at a time to suit the mother. As so little research has been done on the Basking Shark, no one actually knows how long the gestation period is, although the latest research does suggest a period of about 14 months. Amazingly, when the young sharks are born they are usually between 1–1.7m (3.3–5.5ft) long, which makes Basking Shark pups larger than

OPPOSITE *The classic image of a Basking Shark will always be head-on with the mouth open wide.*

ABOVE TOP *Whilst there are strict rules on how close a boat should approach a Basking Shark, they are always on hand to pick you up from the water.*

ABOVE BOTTOM *It is usual to snorkel with Basking Sharks, so as not to scare them away with bubbles, but some choose to go out on rebreathers.*

the majority of other full-grown sharks. More recent research has shown that in the last 70 years or so only one pregnant female Basking Shark has been reported. The conclusion from scientists is that females may well break away from the general population in order to give birth in areas of low fishing pressure.

The Basking Shark is an endangered species which, fortunately, is protected in the UK. They can grow to very large sizes, with an occasional individual reaching over 12m (40ft) in length. When feeding they open their mouths wide in order to be able to gather huge quantities of micro-organisms and this makes for some stunning encounters and great images if you have a camera. They also often feed very close to the surface, so you can watch them from just beneath the waterline, and if you have a camera with a dome port you can get amazing split shots, reflections and beams of sunlight in your photos. Sometimes it is also fun to try to get another snorkeler in the shot to demonstrate perspective and highlight the huge size of these impressive elasmobranchs.

When the Basking Sharks are feeding at the surface you don't even need to pull on all your scuba gear. Realistically, you are far better-off snorkelling at the surface when watching or taking pictures of Basking Sharks feeding in the water. You do need to be aware, though, that the visibility is quite likely to be considerably reduced due to the very food they have arrived to eat, so as you are looking into the water in the direction they are coming from, they just appear to loom into focus from out of the gloom. The best approach is to watch them by looking above the surface for their dorsal fins poking out of the water, as they swim along hoovering up the plankton. It is

ABOVE *A Basking Shark swims past a snorkeler in Cornwall.*
OVERLEAF *The Basking Shark is the second largest fish after the Whale Shark, but this species is found in much colder waters.*

best if you do not try swimming after them, chasing them to get a closer look, as they are deceptively quick through the water and certainly much faster than you are. Trying to pursue them will chase them away and also leave everyone else in your group disappointed. The ideal method to get the best sighting of these harmless sharks is to hover in the water, wait patiently and work out their pattern of feeding and swimming; they will come right up to you if you get it right.

Of course, you can come across a Basking Shark pretty much anywhere along the south-western and western coastline of the UK over the summer months, but to get the ultimate experience it is best to go on a specialist trip – this is the best way to see them in the water, or to give yourself the best chance to photograph them. Most of the operators that specialise in Basking Shark trips are not only knowledgeable about the animal, but also are most likely to know the best places to watch them. You will generally need to book spaces on these trips well in advance as this is a popular subject for wildlife-watching and underwater photography. Of course, nothing is guaranteed when it comes to wildlife diving and photography and you will need to have a bit of luck on your side to get good weather conditions

West Coast
UK

KEY SPECIES
Basking Shark (*Cetorhinus maximus*).

BEST TIME TO VISIT
Basking Sharks usually visit UK waters from April to September, with July and August seeing peak numbers in Scotland. May and June are the optimum months for more southern waters.

TIPS FOR VISITORS
You may want to book more than one day of Basking Shark excursion, as the British weather can be unreliable even in summer months. Make sure that you are comfortable snorkelling before going out on one of these trips.

EQUIPMENT TO TAKE
The water will be cool, so thick wetsuit or a drysuit, and a hood and gloves will be required. Have a snorkel attached to your mask. Take warm, waterproof clothing to wear once back on the boat and for the journey home.

ALTERNATIVE TOP DIVE SITES
While Basking Sharks can be found in cool water all over the world, it is only Scotland and Cornwall that have created a tourist industry around getting divers in the water with them.

and for the Basking Sharks to be feeding inshore. If the wind is kicking up the surface it can be very difficult to spot the dorsal fins moving through the water, so calm, flat sea conditions are desirable.

If you are looking for some tips on how to get some really great Basking Shark images, then you should use a wide-angle lens or even a fisheye if you have one. These sharks are very big animals and will approach you very closely, just veering off at a slight angle as they get within a few inches of you, particularly if you are having a lucky day. Watch out for backscatter if you are using strobes as there are lots of particles in the water and these are, of course, what the sharks are here to feed on. Try natural light shots to get the sun beams bursting through the water. Going strobe-less will also reduce the chance of any backscatter and your whole camera rig will be more manoeuvrable. As they feed very close to the surface there should be lots of available light and therefore strobes or video lights are just not necessary. There is still plenty of colour (even red!). Take lots of photos and stay in the water with them as long as you can – it is a privilege and a special event.

LEFT TOP *Sunlight dances across the large back of the Basking Shark as it swims under the snorkelers.*

LEFT MIDDLE *Basking Sharks filter feed and on a sunny day will be brought close to the surface by their food source.*

ABOVE BOTTOM *A Basking Shark feeds on plankton, mouth wide open.*

The Blue Sharks of Penzance

There are many places around the world where you can see Blue Sharks, but over the last few years one of the most consistent and easy locations to get in the water and interact with them is off Penzance in Cornwall, at the south-western tip of the United Kingdom.

Historically, Cornwall, and Penzance in particular, has a fascinating seafaring history and many places you go are linked to tales of smuggling in centuries past. Just one look at the coastline and you will see why this place was so popular with the smugglers trying to sneak their contraband past the customs and excise officers, who were plentiful in this part of the country.

The weather can be unforgiving as this long peninsular juts out into the North Atlantic Ocean and many divers come here just to dive the wrecks, both ancient and modern – and there are plenty of them. The weather here can also be glorious as Cornwall is the most southerly region of mainland Britain. And when the sun shines and the wind is calm, the climate could be almost Caribbean.

Of all the sharks to be in the water with, the Blues are amongst the most elegant and relaxed of all the species. Their laconic easy motion as they circle and interact with divers is unusual for a shark species, and it is almost as if they actually want to play with you. However, like any shark, in order to be able to attract them in the first place some form of enticement is required. The operators in Cornwall use frozen, pulped mackerel, which they hang off the back of the boat in a net bag. Atlantic Mackerel (*Scomber scombrus*) is the principal prey of the Blue Sharks in this region. On most occasions it doesn't usually take too long before the first of those familiar dorsal fins appear around the boat, circling slowly, but they can be a bit skittish at first. You will need to enter the water as gently and quietly possible, but once you're in and the curious sharks start to investigate you, your interactions with them should be a particularly rewarding experience.

The Blue Shark is a slim and graceful shark with a long, conical snout, large dark eyes and curved triangular upper teeth, which have serrated edges. The pectoral fins are long and narrow with no inter-dorsal ridge.

OPPOSITE *A Blue Shark is highlighted by the sun's rays as it swims under a small group of divers.*

ABOVE *Blue Sharks are curious and will approach closely without fear.*

OPPOSITE *Near the surface the sunlight can create a dappled effect on the Blue Shark. The best trips are when the sun is out and the water is calm.*

For the most part, Blue Sharks tend to inhabit the cooler temperate waters of higher latitudes. The species can be found in tropical seas, although it tends to stay deeper where the water is colder. The Blue Shark is a requiem shark belonging to the family Carchardinidae. Like most of this family it is viviparous and has been recorded as giving birth to up to 135 live young after a gestation period of 9–12 months. The number of pups generally depends upon the size of the female parent and the normal number is around 25–50 in a litter. Blue Sharks become sexually mature at around five years old and can live as long as 20 years. They are often regarded as lethargic animals due to the fact that they tend to cruise slowly in the water, conserving their energy for when they find prey. They are, however, capable of rapid acceleration and sustained high-speed, although they generally circle their prey before moving in for a kill. Their prey generally consists of items such as small fish, octopus, lobster, shrimp, crab and squid, but they have been known to take larger prey and will feed on any carrion that they may find, including seabirds and whale and porpoise meat and blubber. They will pursue larger fish and their sharp, triangular, saw-edged teeth are perfectly designed for grasping such prey.

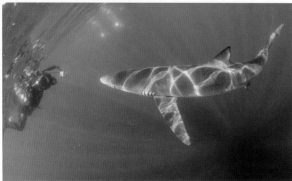

Being in the water with Blue Sharks is a delight. They are inquisitive and slow-moving but they do have an unnerving habit of suddenly appearing in front of your mask, as if they are peering into your eyes, as they come from behind to investigate you. Their huge eyes are endearing and are probably this size to allow them to see in some of the deeper waters that they often frequent, particularly in warm regions. However, they are unlikely to do you any harm. In fact, in over 450 years, there have only been four recorded fatal attacks by Blue Sharks on humans. Non-fatal biting is also a very rare occurrence and is usually accidental – in that same timescale only 13 biting incidents have been recorded.

As the name suggests they are blue, and like many sharks they are countershaded with the top of the body being a much deeper blue than the underside, which is almost white. One of the outstanding features for recognizing this particular shark is its elongated and slender build. It is particularly well streamlined with large pectoral fins, like many of the pelagic sharks. The smaller males are about 1.8–2.8m (6–9ft) long, and the larger females commonly grow to 2–3.5m (6.5–11.5ft).

Courtship is somewhat different to the larger species of shark and is believed to involve biting by the male, and mature specimens can be accurately sexed according to the presence or absence of bite scarring inflicted during mating. Female Blue Sharks have adapted to this mating ritual by developing skin which is three times as thick as the male's.

ABOVE TOP *There are very few encounters that get you so close to a shark species in the wild.*

ABOVE BOTTOM *The Blue Shark will be attracted to the surface and so you only need to be snorkeling to get a great encounter.*

OPPOSITE TOP *Blue Sharks are relatively small and have a beautiful blue coloration on their backs from which they get their name.*

OPPOSITE BOTTOM *Blue Sharks can also be photographed by simply hanging over the side of the boat – you do not even have to get into the water.*

Cornwall
UK

KEY SPECIES
Blue Shark (*Prionace glauca*).

BEST TIME TO VISIT
The Blue Sharks venture into shallower waters around the Cornish coastline in the summer months. The only months to do these dives are from July to October.

TIPS FOR VISITORS
Good weather is the key to having a great Blue Shark experience as calm seas are required, so it is worth booking several days to ensure you get the experience you want. If the conditions are too rough, the diving will be cancelled. As there is smelly chum in the water and you may have to sit on the boat for a few hours waiting for the sharks, if you suffer from seasickness, ensure you take your remedy at the correct time.

EQUIPMENT TO TAKE
A thick wetsuit or drysuit are required with water temperatures reaching a maximum of only 20°C (68°F). You will also need hood and gloves. As you will be out on the boat all day, you will want refreshments, sunscreen, hat and warm clothes. The Blue Sharks are quite inquisitive and will come in close to those in the water, so a wide-angle/fisheye lens is best for photography.

ALTERNATIVE TOP DIVE SITES: The Azores used to be a great destination to see Blue Sharks, but overfishing is sadly diminishing this population. The Californian Channel Islands is a very good place to see them.

The Blue Sharks off the coast of Cornwall tend to be quite receptive to divers and snorkelers being in the water with them. However, they are more likely to hang around and interact with humans who are snorkelling as the exhaust bubbles from the dive equipment appears to put them off somewhat. The ambient light at the surface also makes for great photography and the absence of strobe lighting will reduce any possibility of backscatter in the image. The Blue Sharks in this location also tend to group together and this may well be for hunting reasons. Blue Sharks have been observed working together in a similar way to a pod of dolphins and have been seen herding their prey into a tight group, or ball, which they can then attack and feed from. While Blue Sharks rarely eat tuna, the tuna have been seen following the Blue Sharks to take advantage of this balling and helping themselves to the prey that the sharks have herded together.

BELOW *All sharks are very flexible and can turn right back on themselves quickly.*

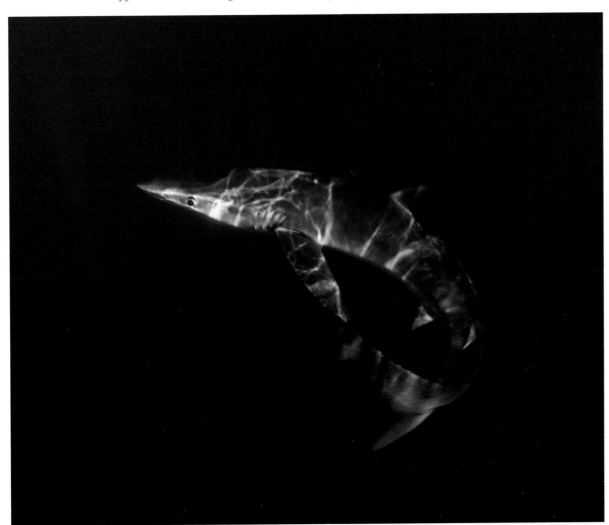

Atlantic Grey Seals of the Farne Islands

Off the coast of the far north-eastern corner of England lies a rugged, windswept group of islands that are home to some of the most UK's most iconic seabirds.

Every year, thousands of tourists are drawn to this rocky outpost to see the likes of Atlantic Puffins, Razorbills, Common Guillemots, Great Cormorants, European Shags and terns of various species. They also come to see around 5,000 Grey Seals which bask in the sun on the rocks, or bob in the water by the side of the boat, beckoning the tourists to join them.

Northumberland's Farne Islands have the largest colony of Grey Seals anywhere in the world and, as divers have been coming to these islands for many years, the seals have learnt to accept these strange bubble-blowing creatures as posing no threat to them at all. The younger ones are particularly inquisitive and playful. With around 1,200 seal pups being born each autumn, there are plenty of inquisitive young seals that are happy to approach and interact with the divers and photographers that flock here to visit. In fact, the seals are so used to divers that on numerous

occasions they will approach you, underwater or at the surface, and consciously interact with you.

You can dive along rocky inlets, which are covered in colourful corals and dead man's fingers, and then suddenly find yourself with four or five of these endearing animals, playing and chasing each other, or they may be snoozing while wedged between two rocks. It is not unusual to be finning along underwater and think your buddy is pulling on your fins; it will probably be a Grey Seal. Stay shallow amongst the kelp or on a sandy seabed, and they might even come right up to you, again tugging on your fins, or even putting their mouths around your camera. The best way to see them is not to seek them out or try to follow or chase them. Play it cool and they will come to you, and once they do, as long as you don't startle them, they will stay with you and give you one of the most privileged wildlife encounters the

OPPOSITE *Some of the best encounters with young seals will be close to the surface where they tend to play.*

76

<small>ABOVE</small> *The dive boat can moor up at some sites in the Farne Islands, but mostly you will be dropped further out from the shallow waters.*

UK has to offer. It can sometimes feel like you are the subject of a competition between these playful creatures. There are certainly some individuals who will tug quite forcefully on your fins, and then roll over as if gesturing for you to tickle their underside. They certainly seem to love nuzzling on neoprene!

Normally, between late September and November, the seals give birth to the next generation and the fluffy white pups can be seen lying on the rocks. The mothers will feed these pups for between three and four weeks, and during this time the pups will triple their weight. The female loses weight and doesn't actually feed herself before the pups are weaned. She will, however, take them into the water once they are few weeks old and have lost their white coat, which isn't waterproof. It is during this period that the mother will show them how to swim and possibly give them a few hunting lessons.

Once this weaning period is over, the pups will be abandoned as the mother will head out to sea in search of food to be able to regain her weight for the coming winter. During this period, the pup, still only a few weeks old, has to look after itself and develop the skills to catch food and defend itself. They are, of course, vulnerable at this point, and if the weather turns, as it can in these rugged parts, the young seals may suffer and quite often many of them die. Grey Seals live for 25–35 years with on average the females living several years longer than the male, largely due to the fact that the males will spend their time defending their harem, or trying to fight for control of one.

ABOVE *There is nothing a young playful seal likes more than to grab hold of a diver's fins and chew.*

The Grey Seal is a member of the family Phocidae – the true seals – and is found on both sides of the North Atlantic, with the Farne Islands hosting the largest colony. A full-grown male, a bull, typically grows to 2.5–3.3m (8–11ft) and weighs between 170–310kg (375–685lb). The females, or cows, are much smaller, at around 1.6–2m (5.2–6.5ft) and weighing around 100–190kg (220–420lb).

The Grey Seal's diet principally comprises fish, for which they will dive to depths of 70m (230ft) or more. Where sand eels are available they appear to be a favourite delicacy and they have also been known to eat octopus or lobster as part of their average daily food intake of around 5kg (11lb). It has recently been observed that they will also feed on large animals such as Harbour

Seals and porpoises, so they are no mean predator. For many years Grey Seals were hunted in Europe and North America for their meat, oil and skins. In the UK they are protected under the 1970 Conservation of Seals Act. Despite this, fishermen off the north-east coast have been allowed to carry out a controlled annual cull, although in the process they are killing mothers in breeding season, leaving large numbers of pups to die. They claim, with very little evidence, that stocks of fish have declined due to the presence of the seals. They refuse to accept that their over-fishing methods were almost certainly the main reason for the lack of fish.

Diving on the Farne Islands is not only about the seals. The area also offers great marine scenery with gullies lined with hundreds of anemones, juvenile fish

and crustaceans hiding amongst the kelp forests. This stretch of coast is particularly treacherous, and as a result there are many wrecks to explore should you grow tired of playing with the seals. Indeed, in several of the wrecks, you may be fortunate enough to find seals hunting while you explore the twisted wreckage. To really enhance the possibility of observing the seals up close, and to extend your dive time, it is best to stay in the relatively shallow water, although this is not always the case. We have had seals playing with us at 18m (60ft), but of course your air and no-deco time are reduced. One of our favourites islands is Little Harcar, where diving along a small, shallow wall, to a maximum depth of about 10m (33ft), your initial encounter may well be with a larger seal buzzing you, flashing past far too quickly to even raise your camera to try to get a shot. Gullies in the rock face are a good place to explore, and you will often see the seals playing overhead. Keep going and you will enter a small bay area, which is where all the serious action happens. This is an area where the seals like to relax by wedging themselves in one of the many cracks in the rock for a bit of shut-eye. The young ones are most likely to be awake and up for a bit of fun, and they will follow you for a while, occasionally grabbing your fin, until they pluck up the courage to come around and have a good look at you. It is the sort of place that can have you staying in the water for well over an hour, regardless of the cool water.

It is important that you use an experienced skipper to navigate around the islands. Its one thing to see the seals' heads bobbing in the water close to the islands, but it is another matter to assess the currents, tides and whether the seals look like they are in the right frame of mind for a spot of playing about with

ABOVE TOP *Colourful corals and anemones cover the shallow reef walls.*

ABOVE BOTTOM *A young seal pup stops as it sees a diver and raises a fin.*

OPPOSITE *Sometimes the best place to see the seals playing is in shallow water which is just a couple of metres deep.*

Farne Islands
UK

KEY SPECIES
Grey Seal (*Halichoerus grypus*).

BEST TIME TO VISIT
The Farne Islands are in the North Sea and can be difficult to dive during the winter months due to storms and high seas, so you are best sticking to diving here between April and October. The best time to dive here is in late summer and early autumn (September and October) when the young seals are at their most inquisitive.

TIPS FOR VISITORS
For the best seal experiences do not chase the seals – it is best to wait at the surface or in shallow water for them to come and find you.

EQUIPMENT TO TAKE
The water temperature in the North Sea rarely exceeds 15°C (59°F) so you need to be comfortable diving in a drysuit. You will also need thick hood and gloves. Underwater photographers will want a wide-angle lens, as the seals come in very close when they are in a playful mood.

ALTERNATIVE TOP DIVE SITES
Elsewhere in the UK divers can have great encounters with Grey Seals on Lundy Island, Devon, and Puffin Island, Anglesey.

ABOVE *The larger adults tend to stay away from divers but the young ones are full of curiosity.*

divers. It is this that requires experience and local knowledge. Just because there are large numbers of seals lying about on the island, doesn't mean they are in the mood for swimming with humans. Most of the islands will have a group of seals hauled up on the shore for a spot of R&R, often after they have been out on a hunting expedition. When approached by a boat, many will dive into the water and then pop up their heads to look at you inquisitively. When there are lots of seals in the water, all looking at the boat, as if asking when you might be getting in, you get the feeling that it is going to be a good dive. At times there may appear to be at least 100 seal heads popping up out of the water, pleading with those puppy dog eyes for you to come and play. As an underwater photographer or a diver, with the sun shining, there is not a better dive anywhere. If you happen to be in shallow water, with playful seals, surrounded by this beautiful scenery, it is even better.

Back on land there is plenty to do in this historic part of England, with the imposing profile of Bamburgh Castle visible on the horizon just along the coast. You can also visit Lindisfarne when the tides are right for crossing the causeway. After a day of excitement, diving and playing with these endearing creatures, most people choose to sit and select from a great line-up of locally brewed real ales served at The Olde Ship Inn, overlooking the harbour and seawall at Seahouses.

The Dusky Grouper of the Medes Islands

There are, sadly, very few places left that have great diving off the mainland of Europe due to the devastation caused by the fishing fleets which have removed hugely unsustainable quantities of the fish stocks over the past few decades.

The Mediterranean Sea is almost entirely enclosed apart from two small channels at its eastern and western ends – at the Suez Canal and the Straits of Gibraltar respectively – and fishing boats have done untold damage to the wildlife of this confined body of water. We have dived in several places on the northern shore and not seen a single fish. There are, however, a few spots that still show what amazing diving there was before all the devastation occurred. These sites are all protected marine parks that have been in place for 20 years or more, and this legal restriction has kept the fishing boats at bay and created small havens for marine life. One such gem is a collection of rocky outcrops called the Medes Islands off Spain's Costa Brava.

This archipelago of seven small craggy islands lies just 1.6km (1 mile) off the shore of the town of L'Estartit. It is, however, the two main islands, Meda Gran and Meda Petita, which dominate the landscape.

The islands do not climb high out of the water but erosion has formed underwater cliffs and caves with the most spectacular cave running through the Meda Petita. The name of one of the caves translates as 'dolphin cave', so named because you will find a small bronze statue of a dolphin at the entrance. As a cave dive it is relatively easy, even for the inexperienced.

The islands were declared a protected area in 1983 and are now one of the most important marine reserves in the western Mediterranean. As the importance of this tiny oasis has become understood, particularly by the fishermen, the fishing restrictions and the area protected around these islands have increased. There are now nearly 1,350 known species of marine life within the marine park area. The waters are fed by the river Ter, which brings organic material from the mainland. Added to that, the upwelling currents from the deep water around the islands bring in

OPPOSITE *The grouper here are completely unafraid of divers and will approach and even follow them.*

84

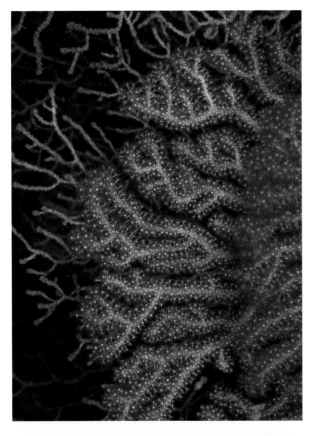

nutrients, which creates a food-rich environment for the corals and sponges that grow in abundance.

As your dive boat pulls up to the edge of the limestone rocks sticking out of the sea, there is no hint of what you will encounter below the waves. They look unimposing and barren from the surface. The water surrounding the islands is usually superbly clear and calm, with water temperatures varying considerably from around 22°C (72°F) in summer to as cold as 12°C (54°F) in winter. As you descend, hugging the edge of one of the islands, the rocky substrate in the shallow water is covered in algae. If you look closely, as you make your way slowly down the cliff face, you can find scorpionfish and octopus using the brown and green plantlife as camouflage. Nudibranchs graze the sponges and hydroids of these shallower waters, or can be seen traversing the algae looking for food.

Descend further, and as the water turns a deep blue and the sunlight struggles to penetrate down to 20–30m (65–100ft), you can find walls covered in the brightest and most colourful gorgonian corals you will see anywhere in the world. You really could be forgiven for thinking you are in southern Asia at somewhere like Puerto Galera or Bunaken. These delicate, varied gorgonians cover every inch of any of the walls that are in the nutrient stream, and come in bright reds, oranges, pinks and purples. It is truly spectacular.

LEFT TOP *Red corals are at risk from poaching in the Mediterranean, so protected areas like the Medes Islands are essential.*

LEFT BOTTOM *Dusky Grouper are threatened by overfishing but are well protected in the Medes Islands.*

OPPOSITE *At greater depths the light diminishes but the corals keep on growing and are very healthy.*

The sheer volume of fish is something you will rarely see in the Mediterranean and it is not only the Dusky Grouper that will come to play with you – you are most likely to see shoals of sardines and anchovies, which in turn bring in the larger predators such as jack, bass and barracuda. It is here, amongst the amazing reefs of these islands, that you will encounter some of the large and friendly groupers that inhabit the Medes Islands. The biggest of these is the Dusky Grouper, which was once described by Jacques Cousteau as the strangest creature he had come across in the sea. It is the best-known grouper species in the Mediterranean and, partly because of its size, it is prized for its meat. You will rarely see it outside these vitally protected waters and due to overfishing it is listed on the IUCN Red List as an endangered species. They are a really impressive fish to find in the Mediterranean and can grow up to a 1.5m (5ft) in length and weigh over 40kg (90lb). They like to live around these rocky islands as there are holes and caves into which they can wedge themselves for protection or use as cover when hunting.

As a diver visiting the Medes Islands you are very likely to encounter the Dusky Grouper and they are happy to be in the vicinity of divers, even approaching very close. This is another factor that has led to its vulnerable conservation status, as spear-fishermen have easily and thoughtlessly taken entire populations. They are now protected in many areas of the Mediterranean to try to rescue the dwindling populations of these regal, though somewhat grumpy-looking, fish.

LEFT TOP *A cactus grows in the Coll de Roses vineyard overlooking the Medes Islands.*

LEFT BOTTOM *The reef is very colourful and is the best we have seen in Europe.*

ABOVE *A diver lights up a grouper cruising on the colourful reef.*

The Dusky Grouper is a protogynous hermaphrodite, which means that each individual starts its life as a female until it matures and grows larger, reaching a certain point when it becomes a male. It reaches maturity as a female at around five years of age, and it is not until between nine and ten years of age that sexual reversal takes place. The Dusky Grouper usually leads a solitary life, lazily patrolling its territory in search of prey, and its diet comprises crustaceans, molluscs and fish. Although the smaller groupers concentrate mostly on crustaceans, as they grow their diet tends to take on a greater proportion of fish, usually reef fish, which it finds in its own territory. Every year, between June and September, the individuals come together at their spawning sites. The females outnumber the males, partly due to the time taken to reach maturity and partly due to the fact that the large males are more prone to human predation. As a result of this mismatch of numbers, the mating is polygamous with each male establishing its own territory and demonstrating aggressive behaviour, even to the females.

Medes Islands
SPAIN

KEY SPECIES
Dusky Grouper (*Epinephelus marginatus*).

BEST TIME TO VISIT
The summer months are the best time to visit as water temperatures are at their highest. The Medes Islands are dived all year round, but cooler waters make it less crowded during the colder months.

TIPS FOR VISITORS
Short boat rides to the islands make this a great diving destination, and one where you can also take in the local culture, food and wine. Take time to hire a car and get out into the countryside to try out the local produce.

EQUIPMENT TO TAKE
A thick wetsuit, hood and gloves are required even in the summer months, and a drysuit is advisable in winter.

ALTERNATIVE TOP DIVE SITES
Dusky Grouper is found all over the Mediterranean, but only in good numbers within marine reserves such as Portofino in Italy.

It is not just the Dusky Grouper and the other predatory fish that make the Medes Islands such a special place to dive. The glorious colours of the anemones, sponges and gorgonians, which are particularly abundant beyond 16–18m (52–59ft), would have you convinced that you are diving in the Red Sea if you didn't know any different. As you stroke your torch-beam across the covered walls, the red, yellow and orange of the sponges, corals and anemones beam brightly back at you. The Medes Islands can truly be described as the jewel in the crown of diving in Spain.

L'Estartit is not far from the border with France and is accessible by road from anywhere in mainland Europe. This means that you can take all your dive gear and camera gear with you, obviating the battle at airline check-in because your luggage is overweight.

BELOW *Dusky Grouper patrol the reefs around the Medes Islands and are popular with the divers here.*

The Devil Rays of the Azores

Sliding off the boat and into the water to follow the action of perhaps over 20 incredible Devil Rays is one of those privileged experiences that will live with you forever. They are one of the great gentle giants that live in our oceans and they do seem to enjoy being in the vicinity of humans.

The species that inhabits the underwater pinnacles of the Azores, to the south of Pico, is also known as the 'Sicklefin Devil Ray' and the 'devilfish'. Very little is known about it and, as a result of this lack of information, it is listed on the IUCN Red List as a species with insufficient data to be able to categorise it. What is known is that the main threats to the species are fishing bycatch and being targeted for their gill rakers to produce 'medicines' that are unproven and unlikely to help with any illness. There is so little information available that even its range is not fully understood.

To find these rays in the Azores, you need to travel 70km (45 miles) from the islands of Pico or Faial. The journey out to the dive site takes three to four hours on a fast RIB, and depending on the sea conditions, the dive boat will secure a shot line to the top of the pinnacle. Very often, for the first dive, it is possible to descend to the top of the pinnacle for a brief exploration of this area before ascending along the line to enjoy the company of the devilfish as they glide around you in groups that can number over 20. The line is there for the safety of the divers as, depending on the strength of the current, it can be very easy to find yourself out in the blue, following the rays in an effort to get that special shot. The dive briefing will always stress the importance to the diver that you must be aware of how far you are from the shot line.

Many divers who have been in the water with Devil Rays have commented on how incredibly curious they are. On numerous occasions during the safety stop on the line, the rays have been reported to circle the divers, often coming in so close that it would be possible to touch them. Of course, one advantage of being in the middle of the Atlantic, where the current can be quite strong, is that you

OPPOSITE *It is possible to see large numbers of Devil Rays on your way back to the surface at the end of the dive.*

may be treated to the sight of other large pelagics, such as tuna, jacks and barracuda, and you can be guaranteed to have the company of triggerfish as you hang off the line on your safety stop.

The dive site is a seamount in the mid-Atlantic, where the seafloor rises from a depth of more than 1,000m (3,280ft) to just 35m (115ft) below the surface. The bank was named after the oceanographic campaign of Albert the First, Prince of Monaco, whose research vessel, the Princess Alice was involved in its discovery on 9 July 1896.

Devil Rays can often be solitary, but more usually they are seen in groups of 20 or more. Research in the Azores has shown that it is rare for larger numbers than this to aggregate, at least on this dive site, although aggregations of over 40 have been seen on occasions. It would appear that the number of individuals in these aggregations increases at the beginning of the season and the numbers slowly tail off later in the year. While research is sketchy, it is believed that changes in water temperature, food abundance and daylight all play a part in explaining the differences in numbers.

It is not known how long Devil Rays live, although there is strong evidence to support the suggestion that they are long-lived species with evidence of one individual being photographed at a 30-year interval. It is believed that they become sexually mature at an age of between 8–10 years old, and we also know that they only produce one pup per gestation. This period is generally unknown, but scientists suggest that it is

likely to be in the region of 12 months with a two-year gap between pregnancies. Like most of the other sharks and rays, the Devil Rays are ovoviviparous, which means that while they give birth to live young, the eggs are retained inside the mother's body until they are ready to give birth. These periods tend to lead to a low reproductive potential and hence the capacity for a population increase is impaired. Because of these factors, there are serious limitations to the ability of current populations to sustain their numbers and recover from depletion primarily caused by humans. The Devil Rays are affected quite seriously by human activity, including fishing, accidental capture such as bycatch, boat strikes, habitat destruction and entanglement in ghost nets.

While the Devil Rays have attracted divers from all over the world to watch and photograph them, it is only recently that scientists have discovered that they regularly dive to depths of nearly 2km (1.2 miles) beneath the ocean surface for periods of between 60–90 minutes. This information was discovered by scientists who tagged 15 Devil Rays and were confused when the ambient temperature dropped to 4°C (39°F). Bearing in mind that these are essentially tropical fish, this behaviour was truly breaking news among the zoologists and marine scientists. Some species of whales are known to dive to these depths but it is unknown among fish species, even the Whale Shark (*Rhincodon typus*). In addition to this incredible depth, they have been recorded making these dives at a speed of 13km/h (8mph), which is faster than any other species of shark or elasmobranch. They carry out these dives repeatedly throughout the day,

OPPOSITE *Devil Rays can be quite curious about divers and will approach for a better look.*

Pico
AZORES

KEY SPECIES
Devil Ray (*Mobula tarapacana*).

BEST TIME TO VISIT
Late summer, when the weather is at its warmest, is
the best time to dive with the Devil Rays.

TIPS FOR VISITORS
The boat ride out to the dive site can take time and might be bumpy if
you do not have perfect weather conditions, so take sea sickness pills
if you need them. If your freediving skills are very good, then this is
a great location to try out freediving with spectacular wildlife.

EQUIPMENT TO TAKE
Even in summer the water can be cool so a 5mm full-length wetsuit
is best. As the dive site is quite remote, take a surface marker buoy
(SMB) with you in case you get separated from the group.

ALTERNATIVE TOP DIVE SITES
Devil Rays can be found in a number of locations all around
the world, but this particular seamount in the Azores is
one of the most reliable places to dive with them.

but spend several hours near the surface warming up again. Scientists have found that the front part of the animal's skull is stuffed with a sponge-like complex of arteries called a 'rete mirabele' and it is only now with this latest research that the reason for this biological heating-system has become apparent. The Devil Rays' network of arteries was discovered nearly 30 years ago and it is believed that this allows the rays' brains to function in near freezing conditions. This environmental adaptation allows the Devil Rays to feed at the bottom of these incredible dives using this well-heated, active brain to forage for the small fish that are abundant in the deep ocean.

BELOW *It is a great way to end a dive when on your safety stop you get a fly-by from these magnificent rays.*

OVERLEAF *These rays gather around the sea mount which is about a three-hour boat ride from Pico.*

ASIA

The Pygmy Seahorses of Bunaken National Park

Bunaken National Park is a marine park in the north of the island of Sulawesi in Indonesia. It was established as a marine park in 1991 and covers nearly 900 sq km (350 sq miles) of mostly marine habitat, with a few islands included under its protection too.

It was one of the first marine parks to be established in Indonesia and this long-standing protection is clearly demonstrated in the incredible health of the marine life you can find here. Bunaken is located near the centre of the Coral Triangle, an area marked out that is recognized as a global centre for marine diversity and a global priority for marine conservation. It is also known as the 'Amazon of the Seas' with 500 species of reef-building corals, 3,000 species of fish and a wide range of habitats and environmental conditions. Bunaken National Park is representative of Indonesian tropical water ecosystems, comprising seagrass expanses, coral reefs and coastal ecosystems. Bunaken lies just 100 miles or so east of the Wallace Line, which is another reason for the stunning biodiversity here. The marine park raises money by charging a fee to each diver that visits and this money is used to pay for wardens that watch out for illegal fishing and diving practices.

Most divers who come to Bunaken National Park are hoping to dive the vertical 50m (165ft) deep coral wall that runs parallel to the island of Bunaken. This whole wall is divided into several different dive sites called Lechuan I, Lechuan II, Lechuan III, and so on, and while they are all very similar in appearance, the treasures that they hold can vary enormously. The numerous colourful corals across the whole park are fed by nutrient-rich waters which are brought in by strong currents, and so you do need to time your dives carefully here, particularly if you want to be able to search for some of the most charismatic creatures that make this unique area their home. There are several species of seahorse found here and they all share, to a certain extent, the ability to hide and blend into the colourful reef. The different seahorse species all vary in size from the tiniest individual, measuring just a couple of millimetres, to the larger

OPPOSITE *At night the seahorses seem to move around more than during the day and are less shy too.*

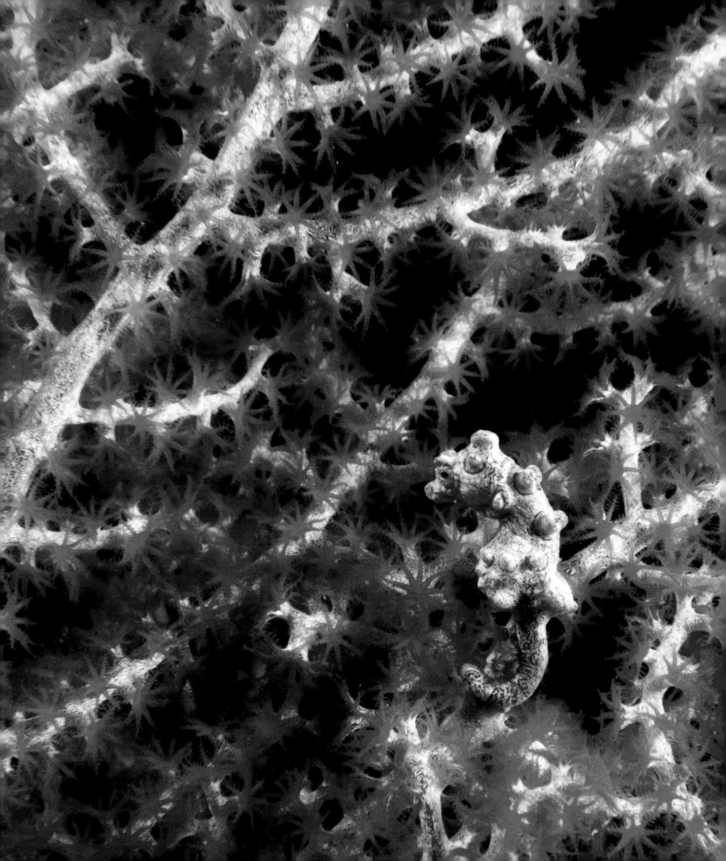

ABOVE *From the mainland the boat ride across the calm seas to Bunaken National Park takes about 30 minutes.*

OPPOSITE *Pygmy Seahorses are masters of disguise and require lots of patience and a good dive guide to even find them.*

species that can grow up to 30cm (12in) in length. The larger *Hippocampus* species found here are the Thorny Seahorse (*H. histrix*) and the Common Seahorse (*H. kuda*). Both of these are usually found at the reef edges, clinging to small clumps of weed and coral near the seabed. They are, not surprisingly, easier to find, as they are larger and nowhere near as well camouflaged as the smaller species. The more prized seahorse finds are those in the pygmy seahorse family, and for these you will usually need to rely heavily on having a great guide, with local knowledge of where to find these diminutive seahorses and great eyesight to be able to find them camouflaged amongst the fan corals.

These pygmy seahorses are found on the reef wall itself, amongst the bright colours of the corals, sponges and anemones that cover every inch of this dive site. One of the most photographed animals in this area is the Bargibant's Pygmy Seahorse (*Hippocampus bargibanti*). They have evolved to perfectly match the sea fans upon which they live and feed. They attach themselves to the sea fans by wrapping their tails around one of the branches and then keep perfectly still, apart from when they are feeding. Each sea fan has a specific colouration, in hues of pink, purple, orange or yellow and the seahorse has adapted to blend in perfectly, to the point that even when your keen-eyed guide points them out to you,

you cannot see them until they make a tiny movement. They are so miniscule that many photographers feel the need to rely entirely on their camera's autofocus system. I find the easiest way to do this is to place the focus point on the seahorse and trust in the camera that it has nailed the image, pin-sharp. This particular species grows to about 2cm (0.8in) in length and has a colourful, warty appearance that matches a disturbed sea fan. The buds on the sea fan will remain closed, and hence the same colour as the branches unless they are disturbed. This way the seahorses are camouflaged at a time when danger is more likely. They often inhabit the deeper sea fans at depths of between 25–40m (80–130ft), so if you are hoping to see this species, it is usually better to use nitrox for the dive so you can increase your no-decompression limit, but do be aware of your depth. It is not unusual to find more than one seahorse on each sea fan, so if you are looking for yourself and you find one, do keep looking for more. Once these tiny creatures have made their home, they will spend the rest of their adult lives on this same sea fan.

The Denise's Pygmy Seahorse (*Hippocampus denise*) is smaller in size to the Bargibant's and only grows to about 1.5cm (0.6in) as an adult. The Denise's Pygmy Seahorse can be far more difficult to find than other pygmy seahorses. It has a smoother and slimmer appearance than its cousin, and rather than only inhabiting a single sea fan species, it can make its home in a range of gorgonian corals. Each of the young seahorses will settle onto a coral and then take a few days to adjust before it takes on the exact texture and colour of its host. Unlike most of the other species of pygmy seahorse, this is the spot where they will live out the rest of their lives.

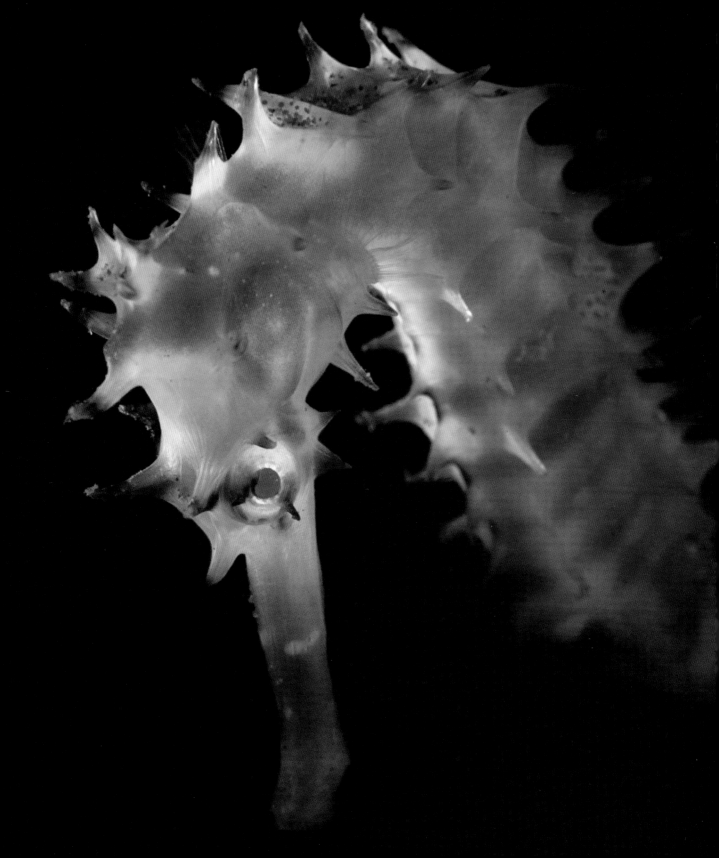

Bunaken
SULAWESI, INDONESIA

KEY SPECIES
Bargibant's Pygmy Seahorse (*Hippocampus bargibanti*), Denise's Pygmy Seahorse (*Hippocampus denise*) and Pontoh's Pygmy Seahorse (*Hippocampus pontohi*).

BEST TIME TO VISIT
Bunaken National Park is a dive destination that can be dived all year round. While the area does have a rainy season from October to April, the seasons are hard to distinguish, so there is not a huge difference throughout the year. The best time of year is still from May to September.

TIPS FOR VISITORS
Bunaken National Marine Park requires all divers to purchase a marine park tag and this money goes towards maintaining this area as an outstanding place to dive. You may not wear gloves on any of the sites here.

EQUIPMENT TO TAKE
The water temperature is usually 28°C (82°F) all year, so a 3mm wetsuit should be fine. Temperatures can vary, so if you feel the cold a 5mm suit may be preferable. To photograph the tiny seahorses that are found here, it is a good idea to invest in a specialist macro lens.

ALTERNATIVE TOP DIVE SITES
Raja Ampat, Indonesia, with its amazing pristine reefs, is another great destination to find many species of pygmy seahorses.

The smallest pygmy seahorse on the Bunaken reef wall is the Pontoh's Pygmy Seahorse (*Hippocampus pontohi*). Pontoh's Pygmy Seahorse is so small and difficult to spot that it was only discovered in 2008. This species is free-living and does not associate with a single gorgonian coral like both Denise's and Bargibant's. They move around periodically, waiting for a lull in the current or surge in case they are carried out into open water. Unlike the previous two species, Pontoh's can be found in shallower water, normally ranging from 5–15m (16–49ft) in depth on the reef wall. Finding these seahorses, however, is a real challenge as they do not even reach 1cm (0.4in) in length as an adult and they move about to find the best feeding grounds. They can usually be found in pairs, clinging to clumps of algae or hydroids, and unless you are specifically looking for this species you are really unlikely to find one. They are white and yellow in colour, have thin, smooth bodies with no warty camouflage like their cousins. They prefer sites that are fed by strong currents to bring in the food for them, and this makes Bunaken a great place to try to find them.

All seahorses are sensitive to bright light and so you need to be careful when using dive torches and particularly if you are using powerful camera strobes. They will turn away from the light and are clearly disturbed when photographed in this way. Many people believe that a decline in numbers is being caused by divers and underwater photographers coming to popular sites like the Bunaken National Park to see them. If you are taking a camera and using artificial light, please consider this and restrict the number of shots you take.

LEFT *Denise's Pygmy Seahorse is more delicate than its cousins and can be much harder to find.*

The Cephalopods of Bali

If you move away from the hustle and bustle of some of the more popular tourist resorts of Bali and head to the north of this beautiful island, you will find the village of Seririt. From the village, a small road winds down through rice paddyfields until you find yourself on the black volcanic sand of the island's northern coastline.

What you can find in this virtually tourist-free region of Bali is one of the world's lesser-known macro dive sites called Puri Jati. It is often called 'PJ' for short and this has to be one of the top muck dives in the world, and also, probably the cleanest. You will not find a lot of coral here, but instead you fin over a black sandy slope with patches of seagrass, where sea pens stand proudly every few metres. Littered across the sand there are large rocks and even lumps of discarded wood that have become home to many unusual species that have made their hideouts here. There is only a single resort to stay at if you want to spend some time diving this great site, but the Zen Resort is well worth staying at. This is probably the better option rather than trying to dive this site as a day-trip from some of the more southern locations. Down on the beach there is a toilet and quite reasonable shower facilities, which were built especially to encourage divers to come to this site. There is a small, local cafe and there are also fresh

water rinse tanks for your gear and camera equipment. In return for these facilities, you are expected to donate the equivalent to about US$3 which goes to the local community and, at least in theory, dissuades people from fishing the dive site. While we were there we saw no evidence of any fishing, so perhaps it works.

Every shell, coconut husk or discarded bottle on this dive site appears to have been acquired as a new home for an octopus, so keep your eyes peeled for anything unusual on the seabed. It takes a while to finely tune your eyesight, but while the seabed may appear barren on your initial sighting, it is actually packed with unusual marine life and juvenile fish sheltering here. Puri Jati is a holy place and so you may come across a prayer ceremony on the beach, depending upon when you decide to dive. It is more usual, however, that you will have the whole place to yourself as this is a dive site that is still way off the radar for most, and you are unlikely to

OPPOSITE *The Coconut Octopus can manipulate items such as coconut halves or shells to form a protective barrier.*

swim into any other divers. Those divers and underwater photographers that do come here are probably searching for the elusive Mimic Octopus. They are notoriously difficult to find, even when you know they are around, and so with a good guide to lead you around, and the option to do several dives at different times of day, your chances of finding one are really improved.

The Mimic Octopus is so called as it is thought to mimic other marine animals. It can change its skin colour and texture like most octopuses, but it differs from the others in its characteristic behaviour of shape-changing. It is the first known species to mimic more than one other animal and some of those that it has been recorded as mimicking are flatfish, lionfish and even sea snakes. The Mimic Octopus uses this ploy for two reasons: firstly, there is Batesian mimicry, whereby the octopus pretends to be an animal that is avoided by predators; and secondly, it uses aggressive mimicry in order to be able to approach prey by appearing to be a non-threatening species. Using mimicry is a common strategy for survival in the natural world, for example, many species of hoverfly have evolved colouration and patterns similar to those of wasps in order to deter predators. The Mimic Octopus, however, takes the evolutionary process of mimicry to a whole new level. It has been recorded as mimicking over 15 species in order to protect itself or to assist in its hunting and this is unprecedented anywhere else in the animal kingdom.

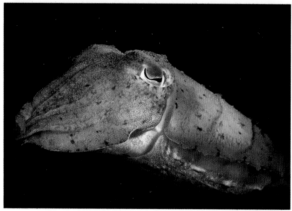

LEFT TOP *A Coconut Octopus makes a shelter from a discarded shell on the sea floor.*

LEFT MIDDLE *Cuttlefish rarely run away from a camera and will stay close to assess the situation.*

LEFT BOTTOM *Bali can offer some wonderful sunrises that are worth getting up early for before your dive.*

Another unusual feature of his incredible animal is that not only is it a hunter, whereby it stalks its prey, but has also been classified as a forager, moving over the sand using its siphon as jet propulsion as it searches for prey in nooks and crannies on the rocks and in coral. The Mimic Octopus is a true carnivore with a diet consisting entirely of fish and crustaceans.

The Mimic Octopus is by no means the only species of cephalopod that can be found in Puri Jati – there are plenty of other fascinating members of the family to be found here. This family includes octopuses, squids and cuttlefish and this dive site at the mouth of a river seems to be a haven for a wide range of species from all of the above. The Flamboyant Cuttlefish (*Metasepia pfefferi*), Coconut Octopus (*Amphioctopus marginatus*), Golden Cuttlefish (*Sepia esculenta*), Dwarf Cuttlefish (*Sepia bandensis*), blue-ringed octopuses (*Hapalochlaena* sp.) and Wonderpus Octopus (*Wunderpus photogenicus*) are all found on this single dive site. These cephalopods are the most intelligent of any of the

ABOVE *Octopuses can be found living and hunting free out on the sand and also in their makeshift houses, often made of discarded rubbish.*

OPPOSITE TOP *Octopuses have the ability to change their coloration and skin texture to try to fool both predators and prey.*

OPPOSITE BOTTOM *Wonderpus and Mimic Octopuses are a treat to find on a dive and will try to imitate other marine life.*

invertebrates. They have well-developed senses and large brains and are known to be able to adapt to live in some of the strangest places underwater.

The Wonderpus is an example of one of the several unusual octopus species that can be found in the shallow waters of PJ. It is quite often confused with the Mimic Octopus as there is some similarity in their colouration and colour pattern, but the Wonderpus has white spots on its main body and its eyes sit on extended stalks. The white spots of

the Wonderpus Octopus are used by biologists as a means of identifying individuals, as the markings are unique. You are unlikely to see both species at the same time either, as the Mimic's hunting pattern is diurnal while the Wonderpus prefers to venture out in the dark of night.

Another amazing cephalopod that inhabits the black sands of Puri Jati is the Flamboyant Cuttlefish, which is very well named as it is so brilliantly patterned and colourful that it is very difficult to confuse with any

Bali
INDONESIA

KEY SPECIES
Mimic Octopus (*Thaumoctopus mimicus*).

BEST TIME TO VISIT
You can visit Bali and the Puri Jati dive site at any time of year.

TIPS FOR VISITORS
The water temperature varies from 27–30°C (81–86°F). This
is a dive site that requires a great dive guide, so make sure
you get in touch with a local dive centre for assistance.

EQUIPMENT TO TAKE
Bring a 3mm wetsuit, macro photography equipment and
a dive pointer (stick) to use for steadying yourself while
taking photographs without disturbing the sand.

ALTERNATIVE TOP DIVE SITES
Many dives sites around Indonesia boast Mimic Octopus
and other exciting species. The Lembeh Strait and Manado
have to be two key destinations for seeing them.

The Flamboyant Cuttlefish is both small and extravagantly coloured and can usually be found on the sand hunting for small prey.

other species. Aside from their amazing colouration of yellow fins and purple tentacles, when they are displaying all these colours can change as waves are sent along the body like an electric light show. They have eight blade-like tentacles, each with four rows of suckers and one of these has been modified to be used in fertilization. As they move over the surface of the seabed, they actually look like they are walking and once they have found their prey, they do actually drop to the seabed and walk very slowly towards their intended victim. Once in range, they spear their victim with the feeding tentacle, which strikes at such an alarming speed that this moment is very difficult to capture on a still camera.

Puri Jati on the north-west coast of the beautiful island of Bali is, without a doubt, an astounding muck-diving site. This kind of diving is not everybody's idea of a great dive but for those who love macro photography or even non-photographers who just love to watch and wonder at the stunning performances that some of these smaller creatures can offer, then it is certainly one of the best, particularly for the variety of cephalopods. It's not just the cephalopods either, as there are many other bizarre and unusual creatures lurking in the black volcanic sands of Puri Jati.

Critters of the Lembeh Strait

In 1859, following many years of scientific research in the Far East, a Welsh biologist called Alfred Russel Wallace was able to deduce that there was a clear division of animal species on either side of an imaginary line that divides the continents of Asia and Australia. To the west, on the Asian side are all the animals, and to a lesser extent the plants, that one would expect to find in Asia. Moving to the east, there is a fusion of species of both Asian and Australian origins.

This imaginary line is now well documented and is known as the Wallace Line, for obvious reasons. It runs through Indonesia between Sulawesi in the east and Borneo to the west. It forms a significant line of demarcation in that most of the mammals and even the birds are clearly segregated either side of the line, particularly the small birds. This distinction becomes even more apparent underwater along this imaginary line, particularly to the east, where you can find some of the strangest creatures on the planet. They only exist in a small region along this imaginary line.

The Lembeh Strait has long been a popular destination for all those divers who love their weird and wonderful creatures, and it is a particular attraction for underwater photographers. There is something very special about this region of Indonesia that makes the marine diversity spectacular. For a start, as already discussed, it is to the east of the Wallace Line, where this mixture of life from both Asian and Australasian origins exists. Biologists refer to this kind of area as a 'zone of transition', and therefore it has a very high number of indigenous species due to the evolution in this region of species-crossover. On top of being situated in the centre of the high biodiversity zone, the water here is full of nutrients both from the plankton, which is driven along the upwelling of the Maluku Sea, and also from the large number of fishing boats that go up and down the strait as they make their way out to sea in their search for tuna. In addition to this, the rubbish dumped over the sides of these boats plays a part in the creation of this unique, fauna-rich habitat. Frequently, this rubbish even creates new homes for the marine creatures and it is not unusual to see fish, eels or octopuses finding shelter

OPPOSITE *Harlequin Shrimp is one of the most sought-after critters on any diver's 'must see' list.*

ABOVE *Ribbon eels come in a variety of colours but the blue and yellow is the most photogenic.*

and a living-space in discarded bottles, wellington boots and other items tossed aside by thoughtless humans.

There are several particularly good dive sites along the Lembeh Straits, but one of our particular favourites for a critter-hunting dive is a location called Nudi Retreat, which is close to the shore. This dive site is overlooked by a 10m (33ft) high rocky cliff-face. You can step off the boat and drop into the water at around 5m (16.5ft) and follow the sloping shelf down beyond 20m (65ft) should you choose to. For us, the really interesting stuff is between 5–18m (16.5–59ft), and this gives the

opportunity for the perfect dive profile for a dive in excess of an hour. Many of the dive sites here have a colourful array of nudibranchs and you could spend weeks just focusing on these ornately-coloured sea slugs. There are, however, so many sites in the Far East that can also boast a plethora of nudibranchs that your time would be more productively spent looking for the likes of Hairy Frogfish (*Antennarius striatus*), Harlequin Shrimp (*Hymenocera picta*), Banggai Cardinalfish (*Pterapogon kauderni*) and a host of other creatures that are rare or non-existent elsewhere in the world. At Nudi Retreat you can find this host of 'critters' or,

more realistically and like most other divers, you could choose to rely on your keen-eyed guide to find them for you. One of the more easily-found prizes, and yet specific to this small area, is the Banggai Cardinalfish, a beautiful black and gold species that forms into small groups and hides in protected micro-habitats such as anemones, urchins and other static organisms that can offer shelter. There are so many different types of shrimp here too, some of which are far too small for the naked eye to make-out clearly. Emperor Shrimps (*Periclimenes imperator*) can be found riding on the backs of some of the larger nudibranchs, not only acquiring free transport, but picking up snacks along the way. Who said there's no such thing as a free lunch? Spiny Tiger Shrimps (*Phyllognatia ceratophthalma*) and Harlequin Shrimps have amazing patterns and colours and are always really high on any underwater photographer's 'wanted list'. If you have a good eye, and particularly if your dive guide does, then both these species are here to be seen. In the volcanic black sand ugly scorpionfish (family: Scorpaenidae), both tiny and large, hide, motionless and camouflaged. They are lurking in wait for their unsuspecting prey to venture within striking distance. As long as you are keeping your eyes open, and you have the creatures' images in your head, you'd be really unlucky not to see mantis shrimps (order: Stomatopoda) and Bobbit Worms (*Eunice aphroditois*) secreted inside their holes waiting to strike at any unfortunate passing victim.

On your first visit to dive the Lembeh Strait you will see more of these unusual marine species than you can find anywhere else in the world. Of course, there are many muck-diving sites around the Far East and several of them can offer a number of species that you may not find here in Lembeh. I don't believe,

ABOVE TOP *Tiny tiger shrimps live on sponges and around the reef and have lovely coloration.*

ABOVE BOTTOM *Stonefish are one of the more poisonous fish to live on the seabed and can easily be missed due to their impressive camouflage.*

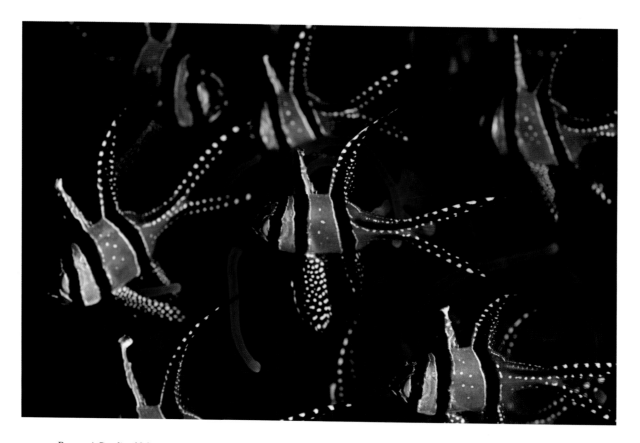

ABOVE *Banggai Cardinalfish are often found living in groups on either anemones or sea urchins.*
OPPOSITE *The Banggai Cardinalfish is an endemic species of Lembeh and is a popular critter found at many of the dive sites.*

however, that anywhere else can offer the sheer variety of species that this stretch of water can. The density and diversity of species is so exceptional that on one occasion, four of our party were together as a dive group and every one of us had found a really unusual and exciting creature to photograph. We were within 5m (16.5ft) of each other and we were all calling and banging on our tanks to attract each other to come across and see what we had found. Of course, we all thought that each of us had found the best critter, but it was only once we had got all

the shots we wanted of our own creature that the merry-go-round started, and one by one, we each pointed out our own discoveries to one another.

There are so many fantastic dive sites along this relatively short stretch of shoreline that it is really hard to say which one is the best. The choice really depends on which of the amazing and unusual creatures you are looking for. It is a case of whether you prefer a nice shallow saunter, gloomy overhangs where you can see the Electric Clam (*Ctenoides ales*) wedged

Lembeh Strait
INDONESIA

KEY SPECIES
A whole variety of critters!

BEST TIME TO VISIT
The Lembeh Strait is a sheltered area that reduces the effects
of any bad weather which Indonesia may experience. This
makes this area a great place to dive all year round.

TIPS FOR VISITORS
As Lembeh is situated on Sulawesi, which offers many other great dive
destinations, this is the perfect trip to turn into a multi-destination package. Take
in another resort on Sulawesi and perhaps even another Indonesian island too.

EQUIPMENT TO TAKE
Looking for critters on the dive in Lembeh is usually a slow dive, and as the
water temperatures range between 26–29°C (80–84°F), a 3mm or 5mm wetsuit
is advised. As you are looking for tiny marine life, a specialist macro lens for
photography and even a magnifying glass are great items to take with you.

ALTERNATIVE TOP DIVE SITES
Ambon in Indonesia is another great destination for critter hunters,
with similar volcanic black sand seabeds and a fishing fleet that discards
plenty of trash into the water. For an alternative critter dive, Blue Heron
Bridge in Florida, USA, is another first-class destination too.

ABOVE *Emperor Shrimps ride on the backs of the nudibranchs that are found all over the Lembeh Strait.*

into a fissure, or whether you wish to drop down a bit lower and go searching amongst the fan corals for the miniscule pygmy seahorses. The fact is, that even if you only had one day's diving at the Lembeh Straits, you could complete three dives and cover all the bases that I've just mentioned. Imagine, then, if you had a week, or even a fortnight to complete three dives a day at the numerous individual sites along this fertile stretch of water. There are several dive operators that are based along the shores of the Lembeh Straits which can offer just this package. There are also other dive operators, just an hour's drive away, at the eastern end of Sulawesi, around Manado. These can offer you an even greater diversity of diving with the reefs, pinnacles and walls of Bankka and Bunaken close to them. They all offer day trips to enjoy the delights of the Lembeh Straits. The choice is yours.

The Frogfish of Lembeh Strait

The Lembeh Strait is a long and narrow strip of water that separates Lembeh Island from the mainland of Sulawesi. Sulawesi itself is a large island, one of the 18,307 in the archipelago that makes up the country of Indonesia [source: the 2002 survey by the National Institute of Aeronautics and Space (LAPAN)].

The strait itself is 16km (10 miles) long and just over 1km (0.6 miles) wide at its broadest point, and both the beaches and underwater topography are dominated by black volcanic sand. Nutrients run into the strait from the rivers that flow through the mainland rainforests and an upwelling in the Molucca Sea ensures that plenty of nutrients reach this narrow and yet exciting dive destination. The strait is a busy route for a large fishing fleet that operates from the port of Bitung, and this has the side effect of adding numerous items of human-discarded trash to the seabed. This does, however, provide homes for the unusual marine creatures that inhabit the seabed; this is, truly, a site for divers who love muck diving. Muck diving is covered in more detail in the previous chapter on the critters of the Lembeh Straits.

Lembeh offers an alternative to the usual perception of Indonesian diving, which is of pristine and brightly-coloured reefs. In fact, on your first descent beneath the sheltered waters, you might be mistaken for thinking there would be no marine life at all. Small patches of coral do appear out of the somewhat featureless black seabed, but you really have to look very closely before the whole area comes to life, with tiny, well-camouflaged critters.

The frogfish of Lembeh come in a huge range of sizes, patterns, textures and colours. Frogfish are part of the anglerfish family (Lophiiformes) and they use a lure called an esca, which they dangle in front of them on a rod-like appendage called an illicium. This reaches out from the top of their heads in order to attract prey and bring them into striking distance for the kill. Some Painted Frogfish (*Antennarius pictus*) are only a few millimetres in length and the largest Giant Frogfish can be bigger than a football, at over 30cm (12in) tall and over 40cm (15.7in) long. Some have intricate patterns that cause them to disappear into the patchy

OPPOSITE *This frogfish has adapted to match the colour of the sponge where it waits for its prey to pass.*

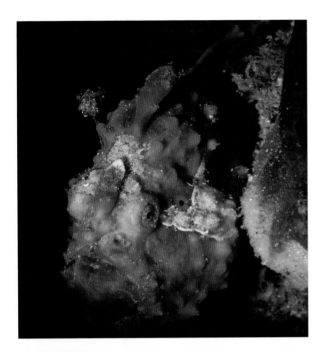

reef, making them impossible to distinguish from the sponges they sit on. The frogfish with coloured saddle-like patches are Clown Frogfish (*Antennarius maculatus*), although this species can be confused with the juvenile Giant Frogfish which very often goes through a patchy, coloured phase. The black ones, in particular, blend in so well that even though you know they are there, you just cannot see them. There really is no contrast at all and this can make it very difficult for a photographer to capture an image when the autofocus system, which is based on contrast, just cannot focus. It is believed that all frogfish have the ability to change colour in order to be able to blend in with their surroundings, rather like a chameleon. Another species of frogfish, aptly named the Hairy Frogfish, can be found in a variety of colours. They are indeed covered in a hair-like substance. Frogfish can be deadly for any creature up to twice their own size, striking their prey faster than any other animal on earth. They do this by taking in water, swallowing it and then forcing it through the gills to propel themselves with remarkable acceleration onto their prey. If a frogfish swallows anything bigger than itself, its stomach will swell to accommodate its catch. Frogfish like to eat crustaceans, fish and even other frogfish. When hunting, the frogfish will stay perfectly still and just follow the victim with its eyes. Once it is close enough, it will move its illicium to make the esca look like moving prey to the victim. The frogfish may move very slowly towards its victim, but often it will just wait patiently until the victim is close enough for the frogfish to suddenly open its jaws and suck the prey into its mouth, taking in the whole column of water which it passes out through its gills.

Frogfish belong to the family Antennariidae and in Australia they are known as anglerfish due to the

ABOVE TOP *Sometimes is takes a very good dive guide to find the more drabbly coloured frogfish.*

ABOVE BOTTOM *Frogfish tend to walk along the seabed rather than swimming.*

OPPOSITE *Their camouflage makes these fish very difficult to spot unless you know exactly what you are looking for and where they might be.*

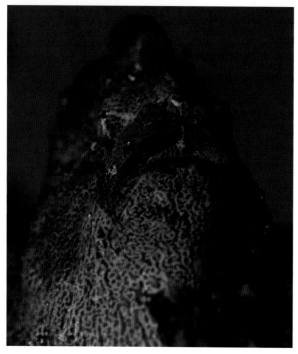

lure they use to attract their prey. They are found just about everywhere in tropical and subtropical seas, although not in the Mediterranean. Despite being well watched and photographed, there is still a lot we do not know about these ugly yet endearing creatures. For example, very little is known about the reproduction of frogfish, although we have had the privilege to watch the courtship by several males of a single female. It was more a display of fitness than anything else. The males were clearly showing off, and the performance all started with one of them sitting on one of the camera housings belonging to one of our group. Another one then landed on a tank valve, before forming up into a line of four, almost as if they were soldiers on parade. During the actual mating process, the female becomes enormously distended as she fills up with huge quantities of eggs. The male then pushes on the female's abdomen as the pair ascend to the surface where the eggs are released and the male releases his sperm. A lot depends on the size of the individual species, but it normally takes up to two months before the eggs hatch into juveniles.

When you dive in the Lembeh Straits looking for these masters of disguise, it is almost as though you are on a miniaturized treasure hunt. You will need to take your time as you gently fin over the apparently barren seabed and this is the key to finding these iconic creatures. The Indonesian dive guides in this area are famous for being able to find these brilliantly-camouflaged fish and sometimes the guides will be pointing at the frogfish for some time before you are able to distinguish the fish from the surrounding habitat. Once you have found them, you can stay and watch them hunt. Frogfish do not move very much at all, as they rely on their camouflage to keep them

ABOVE TOP *Some frogfish are tiny and this one is only just bigger than the pebbles on the seabed where it lives.*

ABOVE BOTTOM *A frogfish gazes up into the water column waiting for potential prey to appear.*

ABOVE *Smaller frogfish tend to be found on the black sand of the Lembeh Strait.*

safe from other predators and also to remain hidden from their prey targets. If you are patient then you may even see them yawn and watching them pick themselves up and walk along the sand to a new location is something you really won't see very often.

Frogfish are usually, although not always, found in relatively shallow water, so you have plenty of 'no-decompression' and air-time to search in these warm waters. A typical dive in Lembeh will see you scouring the black sand for the smaller frogfish that simply look like a piece of broken sponge and then finishing your dive on a mini wall, covered in colourful coral, where the larger species of frogfish can be found. Very often you can discover them hanging upside down beneath an overhang or behind a clump of gorgonians. Once the frogfish are fully grown, they really have very few predators. They are far more likely to be the predator than the prey, although the smaller species and the juveniles can be susceptible to predation. It is very difficult to estimate the number of frogfish globally, but it does appear that

Lembeh Strait
INDONESIA

KEY SPECIES
Hairy Frogfish (*Antennarius striatus*).

BEST TIME TO VISIT
The Lembeh Strait is a sheltered area that reduces the effects of any bad weather that Indonesia may experience, making this area a great place to dive all year round.

TIPS FOR VISITORS
As Lembeh is situated on Sulawesi, which offers many great dive destinations, this is the perfect trip to turn into a multi-destination package. Take in another resort on Sulawesi and perhaps even another Indonesian island too.

EQUIPMENT TO TAKE
As the water temperatures range between 26–29°C (80–84°F), a 3mm or 5mm wetsuit should be fine. Frogfish come in a range of sizes from tiny ones just a few centimetres in size, to the Giant Frogfish (Antennarius commerson) which is nearly the size of a soccer ball. You need both macro and wide-angle lenses to get the best photographs.

ALTERNATIVE TOP DIVE SITES
Frogfish are found in temperate and tropical waters all around the world. Other great places to see them include Malapascua in the Philippines, Blue Heron Bridge in Florida, USA, and Sodwana Bay in South Africa.

they are one of nature's great survivors. They are not sought-after by humans, apart from the divers and photographers that pursue them with their video lights and flashing strobes. Inevitably, wherever there are humans, there is habitat destruction. However, as long as the Lembeh Straits, and all the other muck diving sites inhabited by frogfish, remain popular with divers and photographers, the future for the frogfish looks pretty good. It is a sad fact that this is not the case for many of the other creatures in our oceans.

BELOW *Frogfish are masters of disguise and come in various colours, patterns and degrees of hairyness.*

Manta Rays of the Maldives

The Maldives is an archipelago in the Indian Ocean that comprises 26 atolls stretching over 90,500 sq km (35,000 sq miles). It is situated to the south-west of Sri Lanka and is the smallest of all the Asian countries in terms of both land mass and population.

With an average elevation of less than a few metres above sea level, it is also the planet's lowest-lying country, which is causing serious concern about how it will survive the ever-rising sea levels caused by climate change. Each of the islands is a miniature paradise of palm trees, white sandy beaches and beautiful turquoise waters gently lapping at its shores. As the country is spread over such a huge area, many divers choose to visit one particular atoll and stay at one of the many luxurious hotels that have rooms built on stilts over the calm waters. You can, however, also opt to spend your dive trip on one of the growing fleet of safari-boats, where you can travel from atoll to atoll at the end of each day, enabling you to visit a far wider range of dive sites during your stay.

The diving in the Maldives is famous for its prolific fish life, and these waters are home to over 1,100 species of fish. In 1998, due to a particularly harsh El Niño event, the water temperature rose by more than 5°C (9°F) and this killed over two-thirds of the coral reef. While there has been some regeneration which can be seen today, coral growth is notoriously slow. It is incredible then, that so many reef fish have kept their home here. The waters must be rich with food and the plankton in these waters also attracts huge aggregations of both Whale Sharks and Reef Manta Rays, which feed on these tiny organisms. The advantage of living on a boat, rather than staying at a resort, is that you can try to head to whichever atoll is currently a hot-spot for these amazing creatures. As most of the captains of these liveaboard vessels know each other, should one of them find a group of Whale Sharks or manta rays then they tend to radio their location to each other.

During the month of May, the North and South Ari Atolls are good places to make a start when looking for Reef Manta Rays. Maayafaushi Lagoon in North Ari Atoll is a sheltered, shallow lagoon where many

OPPOSITE *The clear blue water of the Maldives makes these islands very popular for those seeking manta encounters.*

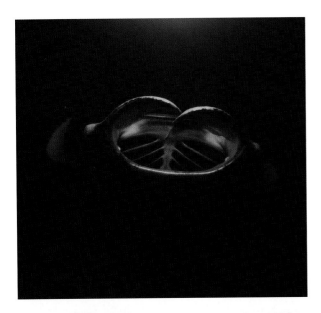

boat captains like to stop their vessel for the evening. By mooring here, and putting on the powerful lights on the outsides of the boat, tiny marine organisms are attracted towards the lights. This in turn attracts the mantas as they have learned that they will find a guaranteed source of food beneath the boat's lights. If you wait until dark and then put on your dive gear and jump in, if you are very lucky, you will find manta rays feeding by circling round and round the back of the boat, mouths open wide to gather in as much plankton as possible with each pass. If you do not interfere with their feeding pattern, it should be possible for you to sit quietly on the shallow sea floor and watch this amazing spectacle for hours. It is surely one of the most rewarding highlights you could possibly encounter as a diver.

A little further south and in another of the exquisite lagoons, you can find manta rays feeding at the surface of the shallow waters, just above the reef-tops, in the full sunshine of the daytime. Because the mantas feed close to the surface, there is no need for you to put on any diving gear, just a mask, snorkel and fins. If you're a photographer make sure that you take your camera to capture some images of a day that will live long in your memory. Most operators will take you close to the mantas in a small boat, and then you can slip gently into the water without disturbing them. They will continue their feeding pattern and are happy to come close to you in the water, as long as you do not chase or harass them. If you try to chase after them, they will move away to a different location and the mantas' slowest speed is somewhat faster than a human's fastest speed – even with fins. Here, in shallow water, the sunlight dances on their huge wings as they move quickly through the water, always feeding with their large mouths open as

ABOVE TOP *Mantas will perform barrel-roll feeding manoeuvres right below the boat light.*

ABOVE BOTTOM *The mantas seem to follow a feeding pattern that will bring them past you on several passes before they change direction.*

OPPOSITE *Mantas will pass over divers and these shots of the patterns on their underside are used to identify individuals.*

ABOVE *The Maldives is one of the world's manta hot-spots and sightings are very common.*

they fly past you. They usually stick to a circular pattern and so if you wait in the same area, then they will come past several times. It is probably worth attending a freediving starter course before you head off to see the mantas as being able to freedive to drop below them for several minutes will allow you to get some great images and they will, of course, be bubble-free.

The name 'manta' comes from the Spanish word for cloak or shawl. The Reef Manta is second in size only to the oceanic Giant Manta Ray (*Manta birostris*), and in fact the two were lumped together as a single species until relatively recently. The Giant Manta truly lives up to its name, as it has been known to grow up to 7m (23ft) across and weigh in at over 1,300kg (2,865lb). Mantas of this size are unusual, but they typically grow to between 4–5m (13–16.5ft) – which is the typical size of a fully grown Reef Manta – and use their large triangular fins to propel themselves through the water. They move deceptively quickly and with a top speed of

ABOVE *In some areas you may come across mantas feeding at the surface and it is possible to snorkel with them.*

around 25km/h (15mph). These large mantas have very few predators. Only the big sharks and Killer Whales have any chance of catching them, and when they do, they are usually restricted to a single bite. The manta's eyes are on the side of its head behind its cephallic fin and the gill slits are located on its underside, which is part of the reason why mantas must always keep moving in order to keep the water flowing over the gills. This means that mantas never stop swimming, either to rest or to sleep. The manta is a cartilaginous fish and is closely related to the sharks – indeed, it is placed in the same elasmobranch grouping. On its upper surface just in front of its tail is a dorsal fin, reminiscent of a small shark fin. The colouration of the upper surface is surprisingly variable and can be black, dark brown or even dark blue. The undersides are usually all white and covered with a few dark spots or patches which form a unique pattern that allows each individual to be identified. If you have a picture of the underside of a manta ray, you can send it to the Manta Trust and they will tell you its

Maldives

KEY SPECIES
Reef Manta Ray (*Manta alfredi*).

BEST TIME TO VISIT
The islands of the Maldives are good to dive all year round and the best
destination to see manta rays will depend on what time of year you go.
The manta rays – and Whale Sharks (*Rhincodon typus*) – move around these
islands depending on where the best food supplies are at any given time.

TIPS FOR VISITORS
Contact your resort or liveaboard to make sure that the time
of year you want to go is the best season to see manta rays
as this does vary. If you are on a boat, get them to turn on
lights for a night dive, which will attract the mantas.

EQUIPMENT TO TAKE
A 3mm or 5mm full-length wetsuit is best for any time of year in the
Maldives. Take a good light for the night diving opportunities.

ALTERNATIVE TOP DIVE SITES
Mantas can be found in tropical waters all over the world,
but some other great destinations to dive with them are in
Mexico, at Socorro and Isla Mujeres, and in Hawaii.

name and a little bit of its history. If it's one they have not seen before, you will even be allowed to name it.

The Reef Manta Ray and the Giant Manta Ray are both on the IUCN's 'Vulnerable' list as their populations have fallen away dramatically over the last 20 years. The impact on such a large animal, which has a low fecundity rate and a long gestation period, is serious. Add to this the fact that when they do give birth, it is normally to a single pup, which itself then takes many years to reach sexual maturity. Many of the losses are down to targeted fishing for the mantas' gill rakers, which are used in Chinese medicine, and despite the fact that there is no scientific basis whatsoever for its healing powers, the demand is still there. Other mantas are inadvertently caught in fishing nets and some die due to marine pollution, a factor to which they are known to be vulnerable.

BELOW *The dive boat can drop you in right where you need to be to get a close encounter whilst snorkeling.*

The Nudibranchs of Puerto Galera

Puerto Galera is just over 130km (80 miles) from Manila, making it a popular destination for local travellers as well as those from international destinations. The whole region around Puerto Galera has some of the most diverse coral reefs in the Philippines and in 1973 was designated a 'Man and Biosphere Reserve' of UNESCO.

The bay here is also listed in the 'Club of the Most Beautiful Bays in the World'. The perfect white sand, clear blue sea, palm trees, a thin strip of hotels and restaurants, all backed onto by the unexplored mountain ranges of the Mindoro make this a stunning location. The increased popularity of tourism in this area has led to a huge improvement in the marine life too, with fishermen putting down their damaging dynamite and nets to switch to a more profitable trade in dive tourism.

Diving from Puerto Galera gives access to over 30 dive sites within a 10-minute boat ride from the beach. It is, however, infamous for some strong currents that sweep over the reefs, and so you are highly advised to employ experienced dive guides who can bring knowledge of when and where to dive at any particular time. As well as amazing fish life, a bay full of Giant

Clams (*Tridacna gigas*) which is guarded 24 hours a day to stop poachers, and a particularly healthy coral reef, the dive sites of Puerto Galera boast over 180 species of nudibranchs. It is this stunning aggregation of colourful and ornate 'sea slugs' that makes this resort such an incredible marine-life destination, particularly for those who love the macro stuff.

The word nudibranch comes from the Latin *nudus* (naked) and the Greek *brankhia* (gills) and describes the fact that on most species you can see their frilly gills sticking up from their backs as they make their way across the reef looking for food. The word is pronounced 'nudibrank' and the plural is 'nudibranks', not 'nudibranches' as you so often hear it pronounced. They are a group of soft-bodied gastropod molluscs and are often simply referred to as 'sea slugs'. Unlike

OPPOSITE *When a nudibranch reaches the edge of a reef it stretches its body out to find another hard surface it can move to.*

their rather drab and unloved equivalents on land, nudibranchs are one of the most colourful groups of animals in the undersea world. They have a devoted following of divers who search out new finds and keep a list of species seen as many birdwatchers will do. Some nudibranchs have adapted to look like the coral upon which they live or feed, using camouflage to avoid predation, while others take on bright colours, which are clearly to warn off potential threats by advertising their poisonous nature. Nudibranchs feed, partly, on hydroids and have the ability to store the stinging cells that they obtain from the hydroids in their body, making them distasteful and painful for any predator to eat. They come in a huge variety of shapes, colours and sizes, with the smallest of them being barely visible to the naked eye and the largest species growing to over 45cm (18in) in length.

Sinandagin Wall is probably the most famous dive site for nudibranchs in Puerto Galera. On this site, corals cover every inch of space, even up to the surface in the shallows, with soft corals hanging out into the current to catch any passing scraps of food. This rocky slope is broken up by two walls, with the larger of the two continuing down to a depth of about 30m (100ft). It is between these walls that the nudibranchs seem to flourish and it would not be unusual to spot over ten different species of nudibranch on this one dive. But, every dive site in this nutrient-rich area reveals yet another species of nudibranch which you can tick off on your checklist.

Look more closely at some of the backs of the larger nudibranchs and you might see the odd hitchhiker too. The Emperor or Imperial Shrimp (*Periclimenes imperator*) likes to take a ride on the backs of

ABOVE TOP *A species of nudibranch from the genus* Ceratosoma *with an Emperor Shrimp riding on top.*

ABOVE BOTTOM *Identification can be difficult as species can differ from region to region, but there are plenty of reference books to help. This is* Glossodoris atromarginata.

OPPOSITE *A vivid blue species from the genus* Tambja *making its way across the reef in the search of a new food source.*

nudibranchs as they make their way across sponges, corals and hydroids. This interspecies relationship seems to be symbiotic with the shrimp lodging with the host and removing any parasites from the surface of the nudibranch. In return, the shrimp gains protection and some extra food that gets disturbed by the nudibranch while it slowly traverses the reef.

The nudibranch has two rhinophores on its head (like fat antennae) that are designed to pick up both scent and information about water movement (currents). The rhinophores have a very large surface area, covered in fine hairs, which are there to maximize the chemical detection process that keeps them close to their food source. Research suggests that the rhinophores may also be used to detect mates. As nudibranchs are blind, relying only on their senses of smell, taste and feel, their rhinophores play a significant role in letting them know what is around in the immediate area. The diet of the nudibranch is varied, with different species favouring particular foods. Many are grazers that feed on sponges and hydroids, while others will eat eggs, small fish and even other nudibranchs. They are all, however, carnivorous.

The characteristic that really makes the nudibranchs special is the amazing variety of their colouration. Very often, the colours can be greens and browns to match the surroundings in which they survive,

LEFT ABOVE *Nudibranch from the genus* Nembrotha *feeding on a sea squirt in The Philippines.*

LEFT MIDDLE *A large nudibranch from the genus* Chromodoris *on the sand. It too has an Emperor Shrimp living on it.*

LEFT BOTTOM Risbecia tryoni *struggles against the strong current as it slowly makes its way across the reef.*

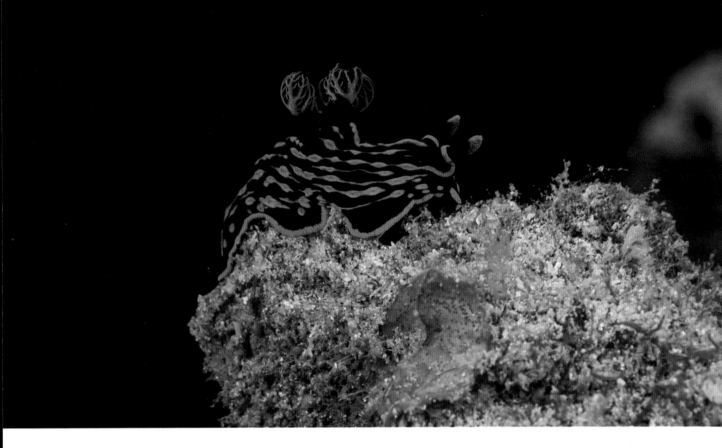

ABOVE Nembrotha kubaryana *is a commonly sighted nudibranch in this region.*

but many shout their existence in bright and gaudy colours that are in total contrast to the colours of their habitats. The bright colours are warning to any would-be predators – much the same as with bees and wasps – a signal announcing 'hands off'. Nudibranchs accumulate toxins on their upper surfaces and can secrete them from glands when they are feeling threatened. These toxins are taken in from the food that they consume, such as the hydroids, and they are then modified and transported to glands on the surface of the skin. This defence mechanism has evolved from the energy-saving transition of leaving their shells behind many thousands of years ago.

Wherever you go in the world, you are almost certain to encounter nudibranchs on the ocean bed if you look closely enough. There are over 3,000 known species of nudibranch and there are many thousands more awaiting discovery and formal description. It has been estimated by scientists that there are probably more unknown species than there are known species. There are many species which are known to thrive in some of the deepest parts of our oceans, but it is mostly the brightly coloured and ornate shallow-water species that we encounter.

Puerto Galera
PHILIPPINES

KEY SPECIES
Various species of nudibranchs.

BEST TIME TO VISIT
Peak season for tourists at Puerto Galera is April and May,
and the best diving conditions occur from April to September.
This is, however, an all-year-round diving destination.

TIPS FOR VISITORS
The local area is well worth a visit, so take some time off from
diving, perhaps on the day before you fly home or on to your next
destination, and experience the local countryside and culture for a
more complete picture of what Puerto Galera has to offer.

EQUIPMENT TO TAKE
In December the water temperature can fall to as low as 22°C (72°F),
but during the peak season months the water is a warm 29°C (84°F)
and only a thin wetsuit is required. As nudibranchs vary in size, but can
be very small, it is a good idea to pack macro photography gear.

ALTERNATIVE TOP DIVE SITES
The nudibranch fanatic is a lucky diver, as they are found in
both warm tropical waters and cold waters too, and occur
in most of the oceans and seas around the world.

Nearly all nudibranchs have a short lifespan with very few living longer than one year. Like the slugs and snails of your garden, nudibranchs are hermaphroditic, which means that they have both the male and the female reproductive organs. This does not, however, mean that they can self-fertilize and this leads to an almost comical situation where the mating couples will often fight to decide who should be the male. Once fertilized, up to 1,000,000 eggs can be deposited within a ribbon-like spiral – a structure often found on rocks by divers.

Nudibranchs are really popular with many divers and in particular with photographers who are new to their hobby. That is not to say that only new photographers go in search of nudibranchs, but as the nudibranchs move slowly over the coral and seabed they are a much easier subject to practice on than something like an anemonefish protecting its anemone, for example. Puerto Galera is a mecca for the nudibranch fanatics and photographers alike, and with such a huge variety of species to choose from, it is not difficult to see why.

BELOW *Some divers spend their whole trip visiting an area looking for new nudibranchs that they have not seen before and Puerto Galera offers plenty of opportunities.*

AUSTRALASIA

The wreck of the SS Yongala

There are so many dive sites around the coastline of Australia that it is really difficult to try and nominate which are the best ones. There are also many incredible wrecks, but it is perhaps the *SS Yongala* that many people would consider to be not just the best wreck-dive in Australia, but probably a contender for the best wreck-dive site in the world!

The shipwreck is 109m (358ft) long and sank in 1911 during a tropical cyclone. None of the 49 passengers or 73 crew survived the tragic event and not a single body was ever found, apart from the celebrated racehorse, Moonshine. It wasn't until 1958 that the shipwreck was even found. To reach it takes a 30-minute boat ride from the town of Ayr in Queensland.

The SS *Yongala* was built in the north-east shipyards of England by Sir WG Armstrong Whitworth & Co Ltd, and was launched on the 29 April 1903. She was purposely built and designed as a steel passenger and freight steamer on commission to the Adelaide Steamship Company and travelled at a top speed in the region of 16 knots. She was quite an advanced vessel for the day with electric lighting and refrigeration facilities for frozen cargo. The *Yongala* originally operated on the passenger routes of Western Australia and the eastern ports of Adelaide, Melbourne and Sydney, but in 1906, she was transferred to operate between Brisbane and Fremantle. A lack of demand on these routes meant that the vessel went back to the Melbourne to Cairns route.

Her final voyage started on 14 March 1911, with Captain William Knight, an Englishman, at the helm as she left Melbourne heading for Brisbane. With 49 passengers and a healthy load of cargo, the ship sailed north for Townsville, but unfortunately, considering the ship was fitted with electricity, there were no wireless communications and despite warnings being radioed out to local shipping about a tropical cyclone, *Yongala* received no message. The ship sailed out of Mackay on 23 March 1911 and this was the last sighting.

OPPOSITE *Huge Shoals of fish inhabit the rusting* Yongala.

ABOVE *The wreck of* Yongala *lies within the central section of the Great Barrier Reef Marine Park.*

OPPOSITE TOP *Divers investigate the wonderful colours of this artificial reef.*

OPPOSITE BOTTOM *A Hawksbill Turtle hides from the current.*

The wreck itself lies in 33m (108ft) of water on a sandy bottom and listing at around 65 degrees to starboard. It is home to a plethora of marine life, including sharks, rays and an abundance of fish species and eels. The top of the wreck is around 15m (49ft) deep, although the visibility is never very good and there is often a strong current, which can make the conditions somewhat difficult for inexperienced divers. Most dive operators require potential divers to have a reasonable number of dives in their log book and require you to dive with an instructor if your level is Open Water diver or equivalent. The wreck, however, is still in excellent condition with many of its artefacts still intact. Penetration has recently been forbidden in an effort to try and reduce the effects of divers' bubbles, which cause a massive increase in the rate of decay of the internal superstructure.

The wreck of the *Yongala* is diveable all year round, but if you want to see some of the large wildlife, then certain times of the year may be more favourable for any sightings. Southern Minke Whales (*Balaenoptera bonaerensis*) and Humpback Whales (*Megaptera novaeangliae*) are regularly seen from late May to November and Whale Sharks (*Rhincodon typus*) frequently turn up throughout October to January. Many people suggest that October is the best time to go as you have every chance of seeing all three of these

wonderful gentle giants. It isn't just the really large stuff either, as huge Giant Groupers (*Epinephelus lanceolatus*), eagle rays (family Myliobatidae), turtles and huge schools of barracudas (family Sphyraenidae) and Giant Trevallies (*Caranx ignobilis*) constantly swoop around the superstructure of the wreck, hunting. Manta rays (genus *Manta*), Bull Sharks (*Carcharhinus leucas*) and Tiger Sharks (*Galeocerdo cuvier*) are also regulars on this amazing metal reef, covered in soft and hard corals with sea fans of all sizes littering the superstructure.

Probably due to the fact that the *Yongala* sits on the sea floor, surrounded by sand, means that it has become the main reef of that area, creating a complex habitat for the diverse range of marine lifeforms that inhabit it. It appears that every possible surface of the *Yongala* is covered in yellow, orange, red and purple hard and soft corals, and the whole wreck almost appears as if it is moving as shoals of fish swoop and swirl around the superstructure. The smaller fish, such as the fusiliers and cardinalfish, aggregate together on the bridge, or anywhere else on the ship that will offer them shelter. It's almost as if the inhabitants of this wreck know that they are in a protected historic wreck zone as they seem to be unconcerned with the attentions of the underwater photographers and divers who follow them to get the best view or shot. If you drop to the bottom of the seabed at

LEFT TOP *It seems that wherever you look there are shoals of fish.*
LEFT MIDDLE *Humphead Wrasse attracted to the camera.*
LEFT BOTTOM *Turtles are a common sight on the wreck of the* Yongala.

OPPOSITE *A moray eel pops out to see what is going on.*

The SS Yongala
AUSTRALIA

KEY SPECIES
This site is a haven for a huge array of wildlife, so
we have not picked a single key species.

BEST TIME TO VISIT
You can dive the Yongala all year round. Each season will bring new
visitors to the wreck. The best visibility is in winter, from June to August.

TIPS FOR VISITORS
Many dive centres will insist that you are an advanced diver to dive
this wreck. It is relatively deep at between 20–30m (66–98ft).

EQUIPMENT TO TAKE
In winter the water temperature can drop to as low as 20°C
(68°F) and so a thick wetsuit is required, in the summer it can
rise to 25–30°C (77–86°F) and so a thin full suit is best.

ALTERNATIVE TOP DIVE SITES
Truk Lagoon, Micronesia, houses some of the most famous and
best wrecks for wildlife in the world, rivalling the *SS Yongala*.

around 28–30m (92–98ft) and look up at the stern, shine your light on its surface and you will see that the colours are amazing and there is also a constant flow of fish swooping through the gap between the rudder and the propeller. As you ascend the more exposed port side, you can peer inside the wreck through the holes, to discover that the toilets and the old cast-iron freestanding bath are still there.

Most of the operators that offer the SS *Yongala* as a dive to over 10,000 divers a year are based in Townsville and it is here, in the Maritime Museum, that you can find out more about the history of the ship. This building was once the office of the pier master, but it now houses, amongst other things, some of the artefacts that have been recovered from the wreck. There are artefacts such as portholes, glassware and porcelain and the ship's copper bell is in pride of place and polished like a guardsman's toe-cap. There is also an old black-and-white photograph of the racehorse Moonshine, the only body to ever be washed up following the tragedy.

BELOW *A diver heads to the base of the wreck, surrounded by reef fish.*

The Fur Seals of Kangaroo Island

Kangaroo Island, in the state of South Australia, is Australia's third largest island and is situated just over 13km (8 miles) off the south coast of the Fleurieu Peninsula. It is easy to access the island by ferry from the mainland, and is one of the country's most popular tourist destinations.

In the past, Kangaroo Island's economy was dominated by agriculture and fishing, but the agriculture never really recovered following the Second World War and now the tourist dollar is growing in importance. The largest town is Kingscote and from here you can pick up land-based wildlife tours to go walkabout in the bush where you are able to see wallabies and kangaroos and visit the huge beach colony of Australian Sea Lions at Seal Bay. There are boat tour operators that will take you out to see dolphins in the wild and it is also where the diving companies are based.

New Zealand Fur Seals, also called Long-nosed Fur Seals in Australia, are found on the south coast of Australia, and there are also colonies on the South Island of New Zealand and a handful of smaller islands to the south and east of there. Kangaroo Island offers visitors plenty of opportunities to see these charismatic marine mammals as they bask on the rocky shoreline or leap out of the water alongside the boats.

As a diver you are privileged, because it is underwater where you will see them in all their glory. They are elegant and agile in the water and also curious enough to come and investigate any group of divers that may approach. Males can grow up to 2m (6.5ft) in length and weigh up to 250kg (550lb), although it is usually the somewhat smaller juveniles that want to interact with divers.

The fur seals are actually more closely related to sea lions than true seals as, like sea lions, they

OPPOSITE *Most interactions will be in fairly shallow water or at the surface.*

ABOVE *Pelicans can be found at many of the jetties on Kangaroo Island.*

have external ears. The fur seal's face has all the appealing features that make it endearing to humans. They have large eyes and a broad head with long backward-sweeping whiskers and a pointed snout. Their body is covered in a double layer of fur which is really soft to the touch when dry. This is the only species that has two layers of fur. The males can be considerably larger than the females, and once mature they grow a dark mane of coarse hair. Around Australia, the fur seals' range is fairly restricted to the south of the country. They tend to inhabit some of the other islands of South Australia and parts of New South Wales, particularly the islands, while there are small colonies in parts of Tasmania.

On Kangaroo Island, the fur seals form breeding colonies once a year. The adult males come onto land first and establish their territory before the females appear, at which point the males then become very aggressive. Some of the sites they choose on the beach can be quite precarious with several of them choosing shelves in the sandy cliffs. Once the seals have mated, the females return to the sea and will only come ashore for any length of time a few days before giving birth. The female fur seal has the ability to keep the fertilized egg dormant for some time and development only resumes at a time that will ensure the pups are born in the summer months between October and December. This increases their chances of survival

ABOVE *At Seal Bay you can visit the Australian Sea Lion colony, which is one of the largest and most important in Australia.*

due to the warmer weather and the greater abundance of food. The mortality rate, however, can still be very high in the young pups. This is mostly due to predation, while their mothers are out at sea hunting for squid, octopus and most kinds of bony fish.

These seals can be unpopular with fishermen due to the fact that they are known to take fish from nets and fish farms, and sadly it is not unusual for the seals to get entangled in these nets. They are really agile hunters and can dive down to depths of over 200m (650ft) in search of prey. Their populations have come under pressure in recent years, but this is principally down to humans and they are protected

under Australian law. There was a time in the 1800s when the seal population went from 100,000 down to 20,000 due to hunting for their fur, and this is the main reason for the introduction of measures for their protection. Their main predators are sharks, and in particular the Great White Shark.

To access some of the best diving sites of Kangaroo Island can mean driving to remote locations via the winding red dirt roads lined by eucalyptus trees where you might be lucky enough to spot a sleeping Koala if you really keep your eyes peeled. Driving some of the longer distances and meeting up with the boat is more comfortable than long and bumpy boat rides

ABOVE *It is a real treat to be in the water with these inquisitive creatures.*

and gives you a chance to take in some of the scenery of this fairly desolate island. Western River is one such dive, where it is much easier to drive through the centre of Kangaroo Island, on main roads, before heading down to the coast. There are good facilities at the beach locations, with showers and a place to get into your diving gear before wading out to the boat to make the final journey along the dramatic, rugged coast to the dive sites. Along this stretch of coastline you can see some of Australia's largest cliffs and they are home to a number of birds of prey that patrol the coastline, riding the thermals above you.

One of the best dive sites here is comically named Pissy Boy Rock. The quirky name of this fascinating location comes from a natural phenomenon that is witnessed here. In conjunction with certain onshore wind conditions, the angled geologic strata in the rocky islets often produce vigorous pumping jets of water spurting out absurdly like a little boy peeing.

The water is cool and so the first giant stride into the water from the boat can be exhilarating. But once you descend and acclimatize to the temperature, you are transfixed by the underwater marine life. It is a

ABOVE *If you stay still and wait the New Zealand Fur Seals will approach you.*

rugged seabed covered in kelp and seaweed that sways with the movement of the water. Large blue gropers are curious of divers and follow you as you tour the mini walls looking for Leafy Seadragons hiding in the weeds. Beautiful 'Old Wife' fish (*Enoplosus armatus*) dart in and out of the rocky outcrops and if you look closely you can find the prized lobster and crayfish that the region is renowned for.

Suddenly, something catches your eye. You can almost sense that there is something watching you, moving quickly but just out of sight. If you stay still and wait, watching the water in the distance, up near the surface, you start to see their shapes, twisting and turning in the sunlight. The New Zealand Fur Seals have decided to join you to have some fun.

The fur seals are sleek, designed for speed, and have an amazing turning circle, so they literally run rings around you. For the best encounters, you want to be in shallow water, within 5–6m (16.5–19.5ft) of the surface. This is where the fur seals are at their most comfortable, able to reach the surface to breathe, and then spin and dive down to investigate you. The more

Kangaroo Island
SOUTH AUSTRALIA

KEY SPECIES
New Zealand Fur Seal (*Arctocephalus forsteri*).

BEST TIME TO VISIT
The best conditions for diving are from April through June. Diving outside this window will avoid the crowds and the diving is still great but expect it to be somewhat cooler and a little rougher. Water temperature ranges from 16–21 °C (61–70°F) as the seasons change from winter to summer.

TIPS FOR VISITORS
Staying in Kingscote ensures that you are close to all the action. You can dive the local pier to search for Leafy Seadragons and it is here that you can get a boat ride out to dive with the New Zealand Fur Seals. Ensure you book ahead, as there are very few dive operators on the island, so you want to be sure they will be open and have space for you before you arrive.

EQUIPMENT TO TAKE
Try to take as much of your own equipment as you can to dive Kangaroo Island, as rental gear is in short supply. If you cannot do this, ensure that you book well in advance. You will need a thick 6–8mm wetsuit, hood and gloves.

ALTERNATIVE TOP DIVE SITES
Kaikoura on the South Island of New Zealand is another great dive site to get in the water with these playful pinnipeds.

time you spend in the water with them, the more relaxed they become and they will get closer and closer. They have large, dark eyes – used for hunting in the darker, deeper water – which make them look like innocent puppies. They will blow bubbles at you, dart between your fins and even come face to face with your mask. All too soon, it will be time to surface, warm up on the boat with a cup of tea and wait until it is safe to change tanks and get back in again.

BELOW *Most members of the seal and sea lion families have curious young that will interact with divers in the water.*

The Leafy Seadragons
of Rapid Bay Jetty

Of all the small animals in all of the dive sites in all of the world,
the one creature I have wanted to photograph for many years is the
fauna emblem of the state of South Australia. The Leafy Seadragon
is just completely endearing.

It spends its life amongst the rack and seaweed of South Australia, brilliantly camouflaged from predators. It is such a bizarre creature that it resembles something that a child may have produced by picking up a seahorse and sticking fronds of seaweed all over it before putting it back into the water. The Leafy Seadragon moves horizontally, rather than upright through the water like a seahorse does.

If you want to see the Leafy Seadragon, then you have no alternative but to go to South Australia to dive with them as, apart from small numbers in eastern Australia, they do not exist anywhere else in the world. There is, of course, also the Weedy Seadragon, which can be found in other parts of Australia and Indonesia, but bizarre and wonderful that the Weedy is, it doesn't hold the attraction of the Leafy; well not for me anyway.

One of the places in South Australia where you are almost guaranteed to see them is at Rapid Bay Jetty, just about an hour south of Adelaide. We went to find them in July, which of course is Australia's winter, and while the water may well have been cool at around 12°C (54°F), we had the privilege of being the only people diving between the pier stanchions. These temperatures are at the lower end of the tolerance range within which Leafy Seadragons can survive. As the seadragons are so brilliantly and ornately camouflaged with leaf-shaped appendages covering their bodies, we thought that they would be really difficult to spot. However, despite the fact that they blend in so perfectly amongst the kelp and seaweed formations, once we had the search image sorted in our heads, we found several 'leafies' of various sizes on a dive lasting just over an hour.

OPPOSITE *Leafy Seadragons will often turn away from you in the hope that their camouflage will make you lose sight of them.*

168

ABOVE *The Leafy Seadragon is the marine emblem of South Australia.*

Both the Leafy and the Weedy Seadragons are very closely related to seahorses and pipefish. The Leafy is a yellow-brown colour, although its 'leaves' are green to help it blend in with the seaweed that it is hiding amongst. In order to differentiate between a Leafy and the Weedy Seadragon, the latter have smaller, less obvious attachments and are usually a red-brown colour with yellow spots.

Watching these endearing creatures propel themselves through the water makes you wonder how on earth they can survive. They have several small dorsal and pectoral fins which oscillate rapidly and this movement propels them through the water, as if they are just moving with the surge. Until you see these tiny fins moving, it is hard to understand how the seadragon transports itself from one clump of

The pier legs of Rapid Bay Jetty promote colourful sponge and coral growth and provide homes for a huge array of species.

seaweed to another. Like the pipefish, seadragons have long thin snouts and their slender trunks are covered in bony rings. They have thin tails, but unlike seahorses these are not used for grasping hold of anything. Instead, they seem quite capable of drifting along on the current, with minor corrections from their tiny propulsion fins and looking very much like a piece of seaweed drifting amongst more seaweed. A full-grown Leafy Seadragon will grow to about 35cm (14in), which is about 10cm (4in) smaller than a Weedy Seadragon.

The Leafy Seadragon feeds on small crustaceans such as tiny shrimps and sea lice. Their diet is limited as they have no teeth and any food that they eat has to be sucked in along their very long snout. Conversely, very little is known about what preys upon them, but it is believed to be principally large fish. One of the dive operators that we went with when we were in South Australia told me that he had been watching a seadragon underwater when a cormorant grabbed it from directly in front of him. It is unknown whether this is common behaviour or just one individual cormorant has learned this approach – it is possible that it was just one incident of opportunism. Many of the disappearing seadragons would seem to be taken for peoples' aquariums at home. It is this practice, along with pollution and habitat loss, that has caused a considerable loss in their numbers and they are now listed as a 'near-threatened' species.

Leafy Seadragons, like their seahorse cousins are solitary creatures and only come together for breeding. During this period, the male and the female hang around together but the moment the young are hatched, they are left entirely to their own devices and the male and

female separate. The male seadragon is then responsible for carrying the young in a pocket on the underside of the tail, where the females use their ovipositor to place about 250 bright pink eggs, which are fertilized during this transfer. The gestation period is about 4–6 weeks. After a period of two years, the Leafy Seadragons are full-grown and mature enough to breed. When the time comes to give birth, it takes between 24 and 48 hours, during which time the male can be seen shaking his tail and rubbing it against rocks. The young seadragons are then completely on their own and survive by eating zooplankton until they are large enough to go hunting for small crustaceans. Very few of the newborns survive, with a mortality rate of about 95 per cent.

Despite the fact that the Leafy Seadragon moves about very slowly, it is known to cover large distances within its own territory. Probably as a result of its very primitive means of locomotion, the Leafy Seadragon is known to remain still for long periods of time, resting in one spot when it isn't feeding. The seadragon uses a lot of energy when moving around, and as the locomotory system is so inefficient, it can really struggle during heavy surge or current. If they are carried away from the reef environment, they will usually perish. They will hide inside the clumps of kelp and seaweed, but with no means of hanging on like their seahorse cousins, their primitive propulsion system is insufficient to fight any notable current.

LEFT ABOVE *'Old Wife' fish gather in large schools at the end of Rapid Bay Jetty. This area is known as 'The Aquarium' due to its prolific marine life.*

LEFT BOTTOM *If you are patient and do not disturb the Leafy Seadragon then it is possible to get very close.*

OPPOSITE *The Leafy Seadragon can be a shy fish and this makes it difficult to find and then photograph.*

Rapid Bay Jetty
SOUTH AUSTRALIA

KEY SPECIES
Leafy Seadragon (*Phycodurus eques*).

BEST TIME TO VISIT
You can dive this sheltered dive site all year around, but the marine life is more prolific in the summer months. The Leafy Seadragon is a year-round inhabitant, but the water is warmer and the sea is calmer in summer.

TIPS FOR VISITORS
The site is an hour from Adelaide and it is here that you will find dive operators to book a day trip. Weekdays are a lot quieter than weekends. While many locals do this dive as a shore dive, try to find a dive boat to take you, saving a long walk with your equipment on, and allowing you to dive the whole pier. A guide from a boat will often search for seadragons before you get in the water.

EQUIPMENT TO TAKE
The water can be cool – it only ever reaches a maximum of about 20°C (68°F) and sometime falls as low as 12°C (54°F). Searching for Leafy Seadragons can take time, so take a warm, thick wetsuit or a drysuit along with hood and gloves. You may also want to ensure that you have both macro and wide-angle camera set-ups as these lovely fish, in this perfect setting, work very well with both.

ALTERNATIVE TOP DIVE SITES
There are other dive sites along the South Australian coastline where you can find Leafy Seadragons, such as the jetties of the Yorke Peninsular. You can also find them under the jetty on Kangaroo Island.

ABOVE *The evolution of such dramatic camouflage makes this fish very popular with divers, but you have to be able to find it first.*

The Leafy Seadragon is a delicate and beautiful creature, but it is now in danger of going into decline due to a shrinking gene pool, loss of habitat, pollution from run-off and being taken by uncaring, selfish divers who want to keep them in their own aquarium at home. If you are fortunate enough to get the chance to dive with these amazing little animals, be careful not to harass them, but hover carefully and be cautious where you put your fins as there may be a seadragon in that clump of seaweed behind you. Finally, as a relative of the seahorse, they are susceptible to stress. If you are using flash or strobes on your camera, please be aware that many seahorses are photophobic and can be damaged by the constant blasting of high intensity light. We will, typically, take two or three images, and then move on and this is a practice that we believe will help the sustainability of any delicate creature, particularly when they are in decline.

The Great White Sharks
of South Australia

Of all the apex predators that can be found in our oceans, I think many people would feel that the Great White Shark is the number one hunter on the list. Of course the true number one, known to take Great Whites, would be *Orcinus orca*, better known to many as the Killer Whale.

Regardless of which of these two magnificent predators you consider to be the ultimate predator, the Great White Shark is a truly formidable creature. While there are a number of places around the world where one can get to dive with these awesome animals, Neptune Island, 40 nautical miles south of Port Lincoln, is probably the most reliable. There are several operators who offer cage-diving in this region, but it is only Rodney Fox who can offer the true expedition experience, heading to the islands for several days and including the customers in many aspects of the trip. Rodney Fox is a man who has devoted his life to improving the image of Great White Sharks since he was attacked by one in 1963. Having seen the effect that the film *Jaws* had on peoples' perception of this truly misunderstood, majestic creature, he felt he

needed to correct this misconception that he had played such a significant role in, as a result of his involvement in the making of *Jaws*. Rodney's son, Andrew, now runs the Rodney Fox expeditions out of Port Lincoln and most of the photographs in this chapter have been taken by Andrew. He uses his photographs to document all the sharks that both he and his customers encounter, for his research.

The Great White Shark is an epipelagic fish which can be found in most coastal and offshore waters where the temperature range is between 12–25°C (54–77°F). One notable exception to this trend is the north-west coast of Europe, particularly around the United Kingdom and Ireland. Very few sightings of Great Whites have occurred in this region and there seems to be no obvious reason for this, particularly as

OPPOSITE *Great White Sharks are large and very obviously powerful but they can also have a cheeky grin.*

ABOVE *Two Great White Sharks swim close by the cages and the divers inside get a great view.*

the water temperatures seem ideal. One of the highest populations of Great Whites, where a lot of research is conducted, is at Dyer Island in South Africa and there are several shark cage-dive operators at this location.

Despite the fact that there has been a lot of research carried out on the Great White Shark, its behaviour and social structure are not particularly well understood. What is known is that where they aggregate, there is a social structure, and that the hierarchy depends predominantly on the size and sex of the individuals. Probably as a result of this hierarchy, the Great Whites have regularly been seen to hunt as individuals, thus reducing the potential for conflict. This, however, is not

always the case as very often Great Whites will gather together in packs of up to six individuals which all seem to get along peacefully. It is unknown whether the members of these packs are actually related, but there is clearly some social hierarchy and structure where each pack will have an alpha leader, which in many cases might be female. It is unusual for Great Whites to resort to fighting each other and conflicts would normally be resolved with rituals and displays. There have been isolated cases where very large individuals, normally over 6m (20ft), have attacked and killed a smaller Great White Shark. These attacks are, however, unusual and it is only recent research, using high-tech tracking devices, that have shown this to be the case.

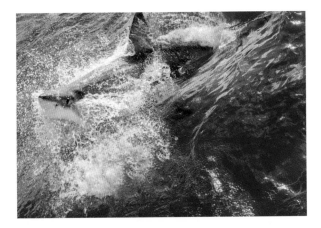

Like the other great predator of the ocean, the Orca, Great White Sharks have been known to spy-hop. This practice involves the shark lifting its head above the surface of the water, so it can look around to search for prey or threats. If you are able to get into the water with a Great White Shark, you will appreciate just how curious these animals are. Having been in the water with the Great White outside a cage myself, I have seen at first hand just how big and powerful they are and how they really like to come in close and check you out. The one thing that struck me more than anything, having dived with numerous species of shark, is their sheer girth and yet it still has the incredible streamlining of a top ocean predator.

What a particular Great White Shark eats depends very much on its size. The juveniles tend to prey on fish due to the fact that the cartilage in their jaws is unable to withstand the impact of taking larger prey, such as seals and dolphins. They generally need to be 3m (10ft) or more before they can take larger prey. As they grow even larger, marine mammals tend to be their main source of food and many have learned to specialize, often depending on the principal food source in the area. Given a choice, like most predators, the Great Whites will take the creatures with the highest energy content, particularly those containing high levels of fat. Great Whites are truly formidable hunters and have a particularly good olfactory sense

LEFT ABOVE *You can get some spectacular views of Great White Sharks from the boat without getting in the water.*

LEFT MIDDLE *Great White Sharks visit these islands all year round but are attracted close to the cages by baiting the water.*

LEFT BOTTOM *In the summer months you can get clear seas, sunshine and sharks that are happy to come in close.*

ABOVE *For a unique view of the Great White Shark you can take a cage lower down and watch them close to the seabed.*

that allows them to detect their prey, such as a seal colony, up to 3km (2 miles) away. When hunting, they tend to use surprise to take their prey. Research, backed up by Andrew Fox, has demonstrated that the Great White will hit its prey, much like the fighter aces of the First and Second World Wars, by coming at its victim with the sun behind it. However, the most usual approach by the shark is to line itself up beneath the target before accelerating at incredible speed and grabbing its prey, and then breaching the surface with the victim in its mouth. There have been sightings of breachings of up to 2m (6.5ft) clear of the surface, a testament to the sheer power of the sharks when they want to move very quickly. Estimates of their maximum speed through the water vary, vastly, from 24–60km/h (15–37mph) but it is probably somewhere in the middle at around 40km/h (25mph).

Recent research suggests that Great White Sharks are far more intelligent than was previously thought.

ABOVE *The sharks come to the Neptune Islands to hunt their favourite prey of seals and sea lions.*

Andrew Fox is probably the person who has dived with and photographed more Great White Sharks than any other person in the world and he has seen how inquisitive these animals are and how each individual has its own personality. When they aggregate and operate as a group, their signalling and body positioning reveal a great degree of sentience, and this appears to allow these creatures to work together as a team rather than attacking one another.

It is known that the Great White Sharks can migrate enormous distances and the monitoring of tagged sharks has shown that it is not unusual for them to cross the Indian Ocean from South Africa to Australia. Other tagging projects have revealed crossings from Hawaii to California and it is now obvious that these sharks are capable of moving not just at great speeds, but also across incredible distances.

Neptune Islands
SOUTH AUSTRALIA

KEY SPECIES
Great White Shark (*Carcharodon carcharias*).

BEST TIME TO VISIT
It can be hard to predict the best time to see sharks around these islands – with climate change come changes in the sharks' movements and behaviour. The warmest water can be experienced between January and May, but many believe that December is the best month to choose. You can visit the islands and see the sharks all year round.

TIPS FOR VISITORS
For the best experience get on a tour that stays out for several nights, rather than a day trip. The journey from the mainland, departing from Port Lincoln, can take a few hours and so a day trip simply does not give enough time in the water. Ideally, go on a liveaboard for three or more nights, so that you get plenty of time in the water.

EQUIPMENT TO TAKE
The water can be cool, reaching a maximum of 20°C (68°F) and a minimum of 12°C (54°F). The cages may be submerged for 30–40 minutes at a time, so take a warm, thick wetsuit or a drysuit along with hood and gloves. Take a small video camera to run all the time, along with your main camera, so that you do not miss any of the action.

ALTERNATIVE TOP DIVE SITES
Guadalupe Island in Mexico and Gansbaai in South Africa are both top sites to see Great White Sharks.

The Great White Shark is currently listed as 'Vulnerable' on the IUCN Red List of Threatened Species and as its only predator is the Orca, all the reasons for this vulnerable status are due to humans. Probably one of the most pathetic issues is the sensationalizing of shark sightings and biting incidents by ignorant journalism, causing a furore of campaigns to kill Great White Sharks. There are also commercial and sport fisheries targeting the species for the jaws, fins and game records. The numbers of shark nets that are set across the bays around the world have, fortunately, been reduced due to campaign groups, particularly in South Africa. The loss of habitat, particularly in the areas where the young and juveniles mature, is also a major factor in the reduction of numbers globally.

BELOW *In rougher conditions in the winter the sharks seem more wary and may not approach as closely.*

The Short-tailed Stingrays of the Poor Knights

The Poor Knights Islands are a group of ragged islands that create a barrier protecting the North Island of New Zealand from the wild Pacific Ocean. Each of these islands has its own characteristics and underwater wildlife and the Poor Knights Islands have played a major role in the human history of New Zealand.

It is believed that when Captain James Cook, a native of my own part of northern England, first saw these islands, the bright red tree blossom that littered the side of the island reminded him of an English pudding of the same name. An alternative suggestion regarding the origin of name comes from a particular view of the islands, from which they are said to look like a sleeping knight.

The Poor Knights Islands are entirely legally protected from human activity as in 1977 they were declared a nature reserve, which is the highest level of protection under New Zealand law. No fishing is allowed and no one is allowed to set foot on the island without a specific permit for research purposes. The islands have in fact been protected for far longer than this, as they were declared 'Tapu'

(taboo) by the Māori Chief Tatua. This followed the massacre of the islands' women and children in the early 1800s. The men were away, having set out on a hunting expedition, when warring tribes from the mainland arrived to do their worst. Largely as a result of the single act of violence, these islands have remained untouched by humans for centuries.

The islands are renowned the world over for their clear, pristine waters. The craggy rocks rise up out of the cool nutrient-rich waters and have been continually carved up by wave action to form a series of caves, caverns and arches which make a veritable playground for divers. It is said that you do not dive around the Poor Knights Islands, but within them, and should you get the chance to dive here, you will understand why. One dive site called the Northern

OPPOSITE *A Short-tailed Stingray scurries away from the camera.*

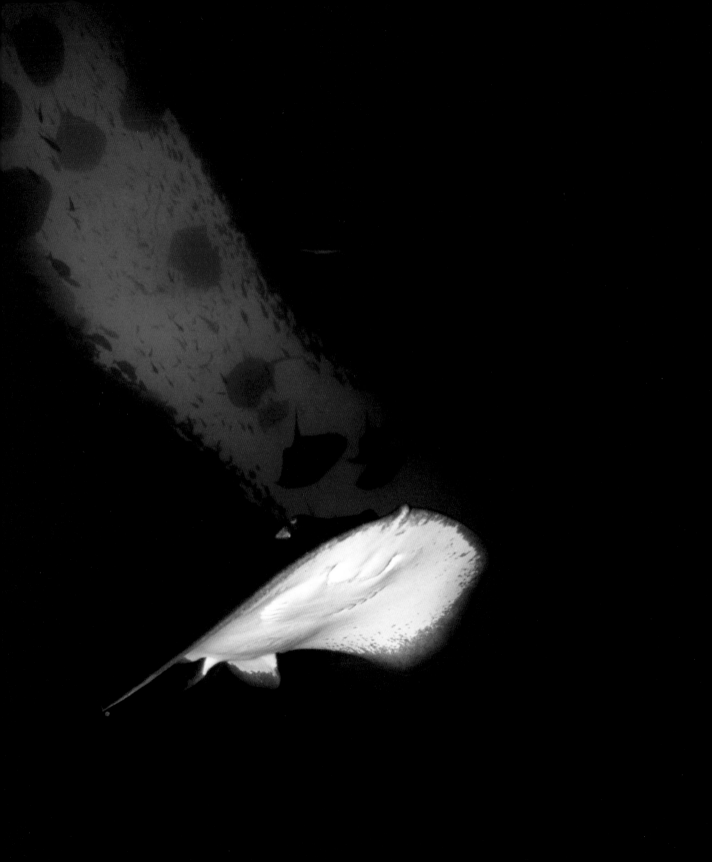

ABOVE *The terrain at the dive site is rugged and inhospitable.*

OPPOSITE *A stingray hovering in mid-water in the current that flows through the archway.*

Arch, which is found off the larger island of Tawhiti Rahi, has a unique gathering of stingrays. Short-tailed Stingrays accumulate in the overhang of the arch that dominates this dive site. They gather together in huge numbers and there is much speculation as to what they are doing here. For any diver lucky enough to witness this aggregation, it is an amazing site to see up to 60 rays sitting in formation in mid-water within the beautiful arch of this dive site.

Stingrays usually have to swim to remain in mid-water, as they sink if they stop swimming and they can often be found, if you look closely enough, resting on the seabed covered in sand and hidden away. It is almost certain that the current flowing through the archway allows them to hover in mid-

water without the effort of swimming. It is also believed by scientists and researchers that they gather here in this way, in such large numbers, to find a mate. Evidence supporting this is that birthing and mating have been documented in the summer months around the Poor Knights Islands.

The Short-tailed Stingray is a large animal and many have been recorded to have a 3.5m (11.5ft) wingspan. This makes this the largest stingray in the world and it can weigh over 350kg (770lb). As their courting and mating rituals have been observed taking place in mid-water, it is thought that the currents at the Northern Arch dive site are perfect for aiding this behaviour, keeping them in position with minimal swimming effort.

ABOVE *Sunlight and crashing seas create a stunning backdrop for the stingray.*
OPPOSITE *A scorpionfish waiting for its unsuspecting prey.*

The nutrient-rich water, protected status, and lack of human interference for hundreds of years, all mean that the Poor Knights Islands are one of the richest waters you can dive in New Zealand. It is, however, not exactly warm-water diving. Even during the summer months the temperatures rarely get above 16°C (61°F) and a 5mm wetsuit, or even a drysuit (for those who really feel the cold), is essential if you wish to spend any time on the dive site. With 120 species of fish and a huge variety of invertebrates, corals and sponges this is truly a diver's playground. You can dive the islands all year round, but the best time to dive,

according to most of the dive guides, is from January to March. The waters here are described as subtropical, as they are not tropical and neither are they temperate.

The underwater topography is absolutely stunning and this means that divers have the opportunity to explore caves and swim through arches, where the sunbeam lighting illuminates the scene below as if you might be in an old English cathedral. Kelp rises up from the depths, and life clings to every available inch of rock face. Moray eels poke their heads from every crevice or hole which has been worn into

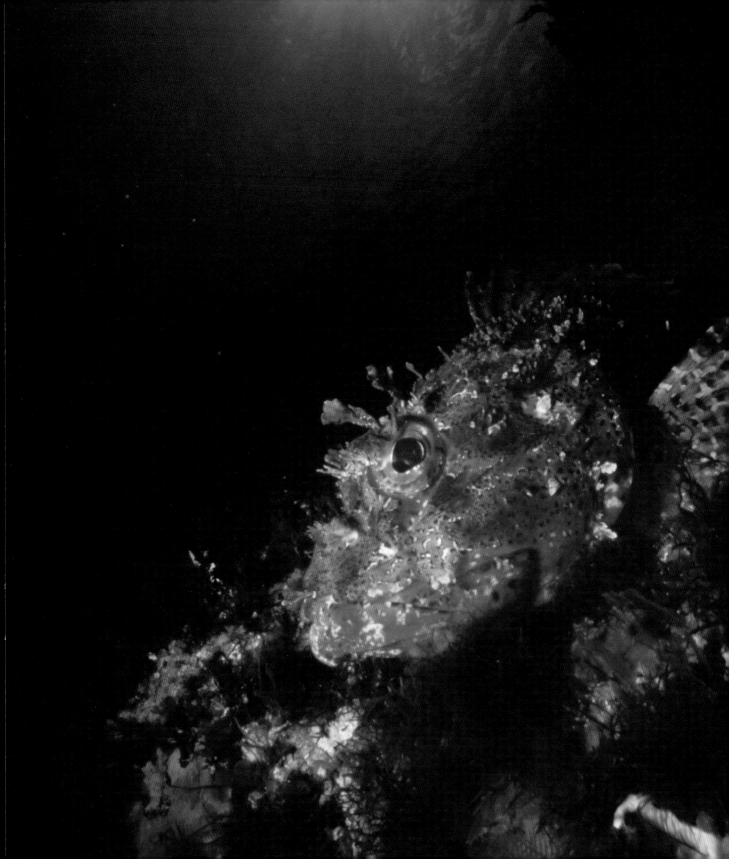

The Poor Knights Islands
NEW ZEALAND

KEY SPECIES
Short-tailed Stingray (*Dasyatis brevicaudata*).

BEST TIME TO VISIT
The best time to see the stingrays is in the summer months (November to February), but the area is good to dive all year round.

TIPS FOR VISITORS
Be prepared for dives in a surge or moderate current.
This is a dive site for more experienced divers.

EQUIPMENT TO TAKE
The water is cool all year round with water temperatures varying between 15–20°C (59–68°F). Being proficient in drysuit diving is an advantage, although a thick wetsuit will also be fine in the summer months.

ALTERNATIVE TOP DIVE SITES
You can also dive with Short-tailed Stingrays along the South African coastline. The kelp forest near False Bay is a good area to try.

ABOVE *Stingrays hanging in the current.*

these rocks by the action of the wild Pacific Ocean. Nudibranchs and particularly large scorpionfish make their way along the reef, grazing or hunting for prey in their search for food. In addition to this, as a result of the currents that bring the nutrients, on any given day, depending on the season, you may be treated to the sight of seals, dolphins, Killer Whales, eagle rays or Bronze Whaler Sharks.

If you get the chance, then try to do at least a couple of days diving here, as there are many spectacular dive sites to visit. You can take day trips out from the North Island, or you can jump on a two-day liveaboard and stay out at sea, to really get a feel for the nature of these islands. If you ever get the chance to dive in New Zealand, then it should be a criminal offence if you failed to visit the Poor Knights Islands.

THE AMERICAS

The Kelp Forest of
Anacapa Island

Along the Californian coastline, nestled in the cool and nutrient-rich Pacific waters, lies one of the most productive ecosystems on the planet, and it is just waiting to be explored. The kelp forest that grows here has a larger diversity of flora and fauna than almost all other marine environments.

The kelp forest provides shelter to young animals from predators, and also during storms. A huge number of organisms can be found feeding here, from tiny crustaceans to huge sea lions and even whales.

Just an hour's fast boat ride from Ventura, across the Santa Barbara Channel off the coast of California, you can find the Channel Islands National Park, which includes 520 sq km (200 sq miles) of ocean and five very different islands. All of the islands have their own charm with wild and rugged landscapes, and amazing habitats covered in brightly coloured flowers and wildlife. There are several species of flora and fauna that are unique to the islands, such as the Island Scrub Jay of Santa Cruz. For the divers however, it is the water surrounding Anacapa Island that holds the interest and, in particular, beneath

the surface of the Santa Barbara Channel lies one of the most famous kelp forests in the world. Anacapa is made up of three islets which provide a total of 8km (5 miles) of coastline. Apart from the kelp forest that it is famous for, the diving around these islands includes rocky reefs, caves and wrecks.

The blue-green water that surrounds these islands is not particularly warm, and to many divers it will feel quite cool. If you want to dive here, a drysuit or a heavy-duty semi-dry is the order of the day, particularly if you are diving it in the winter months. However, if you get the opportunity to dive among the Giant Kelp of this region, which is known as the Southern California Bight, it really is an amazing experience to go under the water into an ocean ecosystem so rich that it has been compared to the tropical rainforests.

OPPOSITE *Cool, nutrient-rich waters make the Giant Kelp fronds grow quickly.*

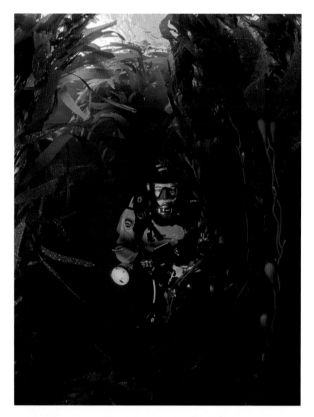

Within this amazing natural environment, there are over 80 species of plants and animals, all depending upon their surroundings for shelter and food. The multitude of creatures that you are likely to see on any particular dive is extensive. Bat Rays (*Myliobatis californica*) swoop and turn between the giant fronds and then sweep low over the sand beneath them. They are beautiful animals that use the beat of their oversized pectoral fins to reveal their food, which can be concealed under the sand. Bat Rays are not particularly large by comparison with some of the other rays, but their wingspan can grow up to 2m (6ft) across and they have been known to live to over 20 years old.

On some of the dive sites, if you are lucky, you may be greeted by one or more of the California Sea Lions (*Zalophus californianus*) or Harbour Seals (*Phoca vitulina*) which have made this place their home.

For photographers, the dive site of Anacapa is mostly a wide-angle experience, but there are plenty of macro subjects that graze or swim in this area. It isn't difficult to spot the Spanish Shawl Nudibranchs (*Flabellina iodinea*) and sea snails which feed on the hydroids and the kelp itself. The former are brilliantly colourful in their bright orange and purple regalia. There are also the Purple Ring-top Snails (*Calliostoma annulatum*) that make their way up and along the fronds covering over 10m (33ft) in a day in their search for fresh pastures. Moving along the sea floor, and very difficult to miss, are the large California Brown Sea Hares (*Aplysia californica*) which have been known to grow to over 40cm (16in) long and can weigh as much as 2.3kg (5lb). Locally, they are affectionately known as 'sea rabbits' due to the shape of the two tentacle-like structures called Rhinophores

ABOVE TOP *Caroline navigates through the thick kelp forest.*

ABOVE BOTTOM *The orange Garibaldi fish are not shy and will approach divers when defending their territory.*

Garibaldi fish stand out clearly, in bright orange, against the green backdrop of the kelp forest.

which vaguely resemble a rabbit's ears. As a gastropod, the sea hare is related to the octopus, and like its eight-tentacled cousin, it has the ability to produce ink to provide a smokescreen when threatened. The Californian Brown Sea Hare is considerably smaller than the Black Sea Hare (*Aplysia vaccaria*), which is the largest gastropod in the world, but it is still the second largest of any of the gastropods.

It isn't just the wildlife that you can wonder at either, it is the whole breathtaking experience of watching the dancing shards of cathedral light as they break through the swaying canopy above and create shadowy patterns that dance across the seafloor. The seafloor covering itself is as a colourful mat, carpeted with stunning bright red gorgonians, eelgrass and hydrocoral. As you make your way through this incredible wonderland of shimmering

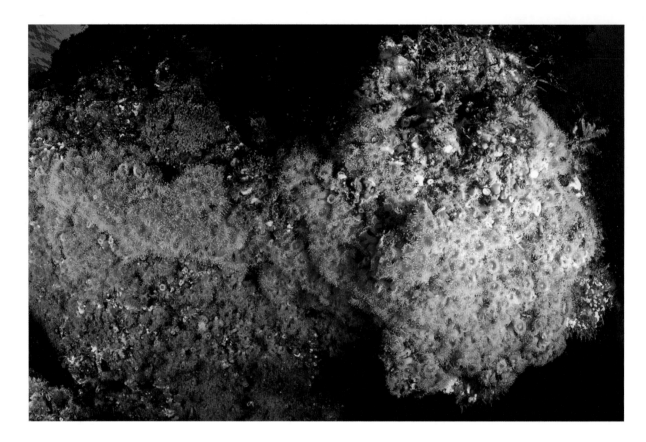

ABOVE *Every inch of the shallow rocks is covered by colourful jewel anenomes.*

shadows and light, you are more than likely to be joined by one or more of the many playful Harbour Seals or even the sea lions that regularly insist on showing off in front of divers. At first, you may just catch a glimpse as they dart through the magnificent forest at high speed, disappearing into the distance. They are just checking you out, assessing whether to come in closer, so it is important to keep your cool and wait for them to make the first approach. As they gain confidence they will come in and hopefully stay for longer. Like so many of these canine-like creatures anywhere around the world, if you don't chase them, they are likely to

approach really closely to you, nibbling and pulling at your fins and nuzzling on your neoprene suit before rolling over on their backs, as if asking you to tickle their underside. They really can be very mischievous and it soon becomes very obvious that you are not the first scuba diver to have had such an incredible interaction with these endearing marine mammals.

The 30 dive sites around Anacapa Island are home to an abundance of flora and fauna. One of the sites we dived held the remains of the steamship *Winfield Scott* which sank here in 1835. Covering

the few metal remains of this wreck, you can find the numerous, small, purple sea urchins which add a little colour to the rusting metal that has survived. Also, beneath the impressive rock formations that overlook the wreck and the reefs, you would be really unlucky not to see angel sharks and moray eels, as well as the indigenous bright orange Garibaldi fish (*Hypsypops rubicundus*) that patrol the kelp, the rocks and the reefs, apparently intent on photo-bombing you should you should dare to photograph anything other than them. They are, after all, the official marine state fish of California and,

as such, surely deserve to be treated with respect. Attached to the rocks you can find bright yellow, purple and red sea fans in near-pristine condition which are often surrounded by a whole carpet of red and purple sea urchins. These islands are also regularly used by spear-fisherman searching for lobsters, and if you get there before them you may get chance to see a spiny lobster looking out at you from the relative safety of a crevasse or cranny.

Other fish you are likely to see are the California Sheephead (*Semicossyphus pulcher*) and Señorita

Anacapa Island
CALIFORNIA, USA

KEY SPECIES: Giant Kelp (*Macrocystis pyrifera*).

BEST TIME TO VISIT
The warmer summer months are the best time to visit, but people dive these islands all year round. To see the majestic kelp forests, avoid diving later in the season when winter storms may have damaged that year's growth. Visibility tends to be best in October and November.

TIPS FOR VISITORS
The easiest way to dive Anacapa is to join a dive boat from Ventura. This means that you can relax on the journey out to the island but be back on shore for nightfall, where there are plenty of bars and restaurants to enjoy while discussing the highlights of the day's diving.

EQUIPMENT TO TAKE
The water can be cool, only reaching a maximum of about 20°C (68°F) and sometimes falling as low as 12°C (54°F). You will want to stay in the water for as long as possible, so take a warm, thick wetsuit or a drysuit along with hood and gloves.

ALTERNATIVE TOP DIVE SITES
Giant Kelp forests can also be dived in Australia and South Africa.

Wrasse (*Oxyjulis californica*), but if you look down, apart from the littering of sea urchins you will see that the seafloor is covered with spiny brittle stars which display an amazing range of colours. We have both seen brittle stars all over the world but never have we seen so many different colours in one location. As a wildlife dive site, and one that is not famous for any one particular animal, Anacapa Island is certainly worth making the effort to visit.

BELOW *Sea hares, urchins and brittle stars cover the seabed where the kelp has not grown.*

The Manatees of Crystal River

Arriving by tandem kayak at a freshwater spring while it is still dark, quietly slipping on fins, hood and mask, and seeing a large dark shape loom up from the bottom to investigate the activity at the surface will fill you with excitement on this trip. Whether you hire kayaks and make you own way to a site like Homosassa Springs, or whether you chose to take an organized riverboat tour to Three Sisters Springs in Crystal River, this is an important moment.

As the sun starts to creep over the horizon you can slip into the cool water and let your eyes adjust to the gloom. If you swim slowly, or just stay still, it won't be too long before one or more curious manatees will make themselves known to you. This is an amazing experience and one of a handful of marine encounters with large species that will allow humans to get so close. An adult manatee can weigh up to 600kg (1,300lb), and these incredible animals have a large boulder-shaped body, flat paddle-like tail and pectoral flippers, black marble-like eyes and a snub, bristled snout.

The clearest water in which to see the manatees is at Three Sisters Springs in Crystal River. The entrance to this site is a narrow channel, and while you are snorkelling into the spring you are likely to be greeted by manatees making their way below you, either moving in to the warm spring water outlet, or heading out into the main river to graze. Manatees are vegetarian and feed, principally, on the sea grass that grows on the bottom of the river, but they will eat other plant material. You may also be able to hear female manatees calling to their calves, by making high-pitched squeaking noises.

Once you arrive in the spring itself you will see steam rising slowly from the surface until the sun gets higher in the sky and warms the surrounding air. Here the water gets a little deeper and, as the daylight takes over, you will be able to see manatees resting on the sandy bottom, occasionally surfacing

OPPOSITE *Manatees often just stay motionless at the surface, although they usually rest on the bottom of the spring.*

ABOVE *A volunteer warden kayaks over the sleeping manatees to ensure those visiting do not disturb them.*
OPPOSITE *A mother feeding her calf at Three Sisters Spring.*

for air. Some of the individuals will come to see you, butting their leathery faces right up against your mask or rolling over in front of you, seemingly asking to be rubbed or tickled. Rubbing or stroking manatees is allowed, as long as you only use one hand so it cannot be seen as grabbing. It is believed that the algae growing on them irritates them and they approach humans to scratch the itching area. This is an occasion to take your time, find your own space on the surface of one of the three pools, and don't return to the riverboat for your hot drink and doughnut until you have had your fair share of encounters.

Manatees are vigorously protected in Florida and there are strict rules on what is allowed on these encounters. There are numerous volunteer wardens patrolling the area by kayak to ensure that everyone follows the rules, and while they may be volunteers, they have the authority to take you out of the water and even, in extreme circumstances, to fine you. No one is allowed to disturb or harass these creatures by chasing after them, freediving down to the bottom of the pool where they are resting, or grabbing hold of them. However, you really don't need to carry out any of these actions,

as the manatees, left to their own devices, will come right up to you as long as you are patient.

There are marked off areas where no boats or people are allowed to enter, and this is so that the manatees have a sanctuary, a place for them to retreat to without being disturbed. Manatees come to the spring waters to stay warm as the seawater temperatures in the northern part of the Gulf of Mexico get too cold over the winter months for them to survive. During very cold periods, which may last several weeks even in sunny Florida, hundreds of manatees can be seen gathering in this area around Crystal River.

One idea that might be worth considering is to think about hiring kayaks. This way you are free to explore all the other surrounding springs, and perhaps find your own manatees to snorkel with and photograph. Be aware, however, that all the rules of behaviour with manatees are still enforced.

Homosassa Springs does not have water as clear as you will find at Three Sisters, but it does offer the opportunity of a great manatee encounter with far fewer people around to compete for their attention. Manatees will rub up against your kayak to try and remove the algae growing on their backs, or even use the kayak's painter line as dental floss!

While you are in the area, these springs have also created some other great sites for diving. There is always the chance that you may encounter a manatee (or maybe even an alligator) during your dives, but these sites are really more about exploring the crystal clear water, the caverns and the caves that have been formed by the action of the water from

ABOVE *The Three Sisters is surrounded by woodland and is a truly lovely place to visit.*

OPPOSITE TOP *Manatees will often swim right up to those that come into the spring to see them.*

OPPOSITE BOTTOM *Whilst it is very important not to chase manatees, you may find they want to approach you and will come very close.*

Crystal River
FLORIDA, USA

KEY SPECIES
American Manatee (*Trichechus manatus*)

BEST TIME TO VISIT
The manatees start to make their way inland in large numbers
as the air and water temperatures drop in the winter months.
The best time to visit is between November and March, but
some manatees are present throughout most of the year.

TIPS FOR VISITORS
Get there before the crowds. This can be a very popular place and so
an early morning start is the best option. Get out as early as you can,
and also try to avoid busy USA holidays and weekends if possible.

EQUIPMENT TO TAKE
The water temperature in the springs is a constant 22°C (72°F), and as
you will not be swimming too much, a thick 5mm or 6mm wetsuit, hood
and gloves are advised. As it can also be cool on the surface, taking some
warm clothes to wear once you are out of the water is a good idea.

ALTERNATIVE TOP DIVE SITES
Homosassa, just down the road from Crystal River, is a quieter place
to encounter manatees, but with reduced visibility in the water. The
close relative of the manatee, the Dugong (*Dugong dugon*), can be
seen with confidence at Abu Dabbab, near Marsa Alam in Egypt.

ABOVE *Manatees have to surface regularly to breathe.*

the numerous aquifers that flow beneath this part of Florida. There is diving for people of all levels at these locations, with shallow easy dives for the novice or less experienced and deep, dark, penetrating dives for those with cave-diving experience and qualifications. Ginnie Spring and Manatee Spring are just a short drive from your base at Crystal River and offer a number of different dive experiences. Rainbow River, too, is a fauna-packed shallow drift dive full of terrapins and freshwater fish you are unlikely to see so clearly anywhere else.

This area of Florida is perfect for a family holiday, as non-divers of all ages are able to snorkel with the manatees in water that never gets cold. It also offers one of the world's most amazing close-up encounters with a large marine animal.

The Goliath Groupers
of Looe Key

When I talk to divers about dive sites around the world, if I ever mention the Florida Keys I frequently receive a frown and a look that says… really? Very few people outside of Florida realise that the US government established the Florida Keys as a National Marine Sanctuary in 1990 in an effort to protect the marine habitat.

The chain of islands that runs for 190km (120 miles) south-west from the tip of mainland Florida is the only coral barrier reef in the continental United States. A lot of effort goes into looking after the marine environment of the Florida Keys. The Florida authorities would argue that it is one of the most diverse diving destinations in the world with several excellent shipwrecks, shallow reefs and many deep reefs. All the way down the island chain, there are operators which can offer a short boat ride to the dive sites and most of these have mooring buoys to prevent any damage to the reef from anchors. There are dive sites virtually all the way along the keys, with the waters of the Gulf of Mexico on one side and the Atlantic on the other. The reef system itself stretches out about 8km (5 miles) off the shores of the keys.

There are several famous islands, such as Key West and Key Largo. Both of these offer excellent wreck-diving, but the real gem for wildlife is Looe Key.

Looe Key is a spur and groove reef that lies around 8km (5 miles) off the coast of Big Pine Key. It got its name from a British ship, the *HMS Looe*, which is supposed to have run aground here in 1744 while towing a captured French ship. Looe Key was one of the first islands of the chain to become a National Marine Sanctuary, which was in 1981. Today this reef, which comprises coral fingers sticking out into the sandy seabed, is a refuge for a surprising abundance of marine life. This reef is home to over 150 species of fish and it is also likely that divers here will get a chance to see passing sharks and rays.

OPPOSITE *Huge numbers of these big fish gather in Florida to spawn each year.*

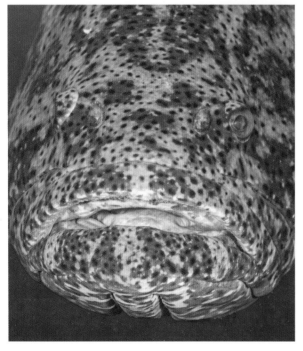

The coral reef growth here is thought to be over 7,000 years old and strict guidelines are in place regarding anchoring boats, spear-fishing, snorkelling, diving and lobster-hunting, in order to try and prevent any damage to this stunning reef structure.

One of the largest fish any diver might see here is the Goliath Grouper, which is a mighty fish and the largest in the grouper family, growing to over 2m (6ft) in length and weighing up to 360kg (800lb). It is a naturally inquisitive species and this makes it relatively easy to approach, study and photograph. Alas, their docile nature has made them very popular with spear-fishermen who seem to think it is their god-given right to help themselves and kill and take such a beautiful creature that we should all be able to enjoy. This, along with their spawning aggregations, makes them even easier to harvest in large numbers. It also means that their population, like those of so many of the other larger species across the seas and oceans of the world, has rapidly gone into decline. Some help is now at hand, with the species currently listed by the IUCN as 'Critically Endangered' and a harvest ban in place in the USA since 1990. Prior to this, the Goliath Grouper had been targeted by both commercial and recreational fishermen since the mid- to late 1800s. They are particularly vulnerable to overfishing, largely due to a combination of biological factors. They grow very slowly and can live for up to 100 years according to some sources, although typically their natural lifespan is usually 40–50 years. They are also vulnerable to temperature stress and if the water temperatures fall too low they can die. Goliath Groupers have been known to form into large spawning groups, sometimes with over 100 individuals aggregating at known sites during July, August and September.

ABOVE TOP *Grouper allow smaller cleaner fish to remove parasites and any other unwanted particles from their skin.*

ABOVE BOTTOM *They are unafraid of divers and are even sometimes curious enough to swim right up to people, which has made them easy targets for spear fishermen.*

ABOVE *Groupers will occasionally yawn and this is probably a warning display to the photographer.*
OVERLEAF *Goliath Grouper are one of the largest of species in their family and they are threatened by overfishing.*

It is during this period that they are particularly vulnerable. It takes the Goliath Grouper a long time to reach sexual maturity and before they are fully grown they are known to be predated by barracuda, moray eels and hammerhead sharks. Once fully grown, hammerheads and humans are its only predators.

These magnificent fish can be seen lurking in the recesses of a shipwreck called the *Adolphus Busch*, which was deliberately sunk here. This wreck is a fabulous dive site in its own right, and at 60m (200ft) in length it requires four mooring buoys along the length of the ship. Two of these buoys are for fishing boats and the other two are for dive boats to attach to. It was sunk on 5th December 1998 as an artificial reef system, largely to encourage dive tourism. The ship is still intact and stands upright in 30m (100ft) of water just 10km (6 miles) south-west of Big Pine Key. Looking down from the dive boat, you can see the tower at a depth of 12m (40ft), and once in the water you will see the main deck at a depth of around 25m (80ft). At the bottom, on the seabed, the ship lies in 35m (115ft) of water with some of it buried in sand which has built up around it over the years.

Looe Key
FLORIDA, USA

KEY SPECIES
Goliath Grouper (*Epinephelus itajara*).

BEST TIME TO VISIT
You can dive the Florida Keys all year round. The Goliath Groupers spawn in August and September and so this can be a great time to visit (but this period coincides with hurricane season which can ruin diving conditions if you are unlucky enough to catch a tropical storm).

TIPS FOR VISITORS
Hire a car and take in some of the great diving that can be experienced all along the Florida Keys.

EQUIPMENT TO TAKE
Water temperature varies greatly from around 21°C (70°F) in the winter months (December to February) to nearer 28°C (82°F) in the summer (June to September), so the equipment you require will be dependent upon time of year you dive.

ALTERNATIVE TOP DIVE SITES
Jupiter, also in Florida, USA, and Jardines de la Reina, Cuba, are two great alternative destinations for seeing Goliath Groupers.

Despite having been deliberately sunk no explosives were used in the process, so 12 large holes have been cut into the body of the ship to allow swim-throughs for divers wishing to safely penetrate the vessel. Peer into a doorway or into the wheelhouse of this artificial reef and you may come face to face with these giant and yet quite docile groupers. Three Goliath Groupers usually patrol this dive site with the largest one probably weighing over 130kg (290lb). Because of its depth, most operators would expect a minimum dive certification level of PADI Advanced, or equivalent, and it is worth considering using nitrox in order to extend your no-decompression time. Apart from the Goliath Groupers, there are plenty of other fish to see on this impressive wreck, including large schools of jacks and barracudas. Swirling around the superstructure, you're likely to see huge schools of grunts as they make their way between the sponges and corals that litter the surfaces of the wreck.

Between the reef and the wreck, it is possible to find over 150 species of fish, including angelfish, moray eels, yellowtail, sergeant majors and numerous parrotfish species. Sharks and rays are regularly seen and, as experts believe that the coral has been growing on this reef for over 7,000 years, you can expect to count about 50 species of coral. We have dived numerous reefs and wrecks along the keys, from the Spiegel Grove at Key Largo down to the one-time missile-tracking ship, the *USS Vandenberg* off Key West, and like all good wrecks they attract stunning wildlife. The diving throughout the Florida Keys really can be very good indeed, but don't miss going in search of the Goliath Groupers of Looe Key.

LEFT *These grouper tend to patrol close to the reef or inside wrecks rather than out in the open ocean.*

Caribbean Reef Sharks of New Providence Island

The Caribbean Reef Shark can be found in any region along the Atlantic coast of the Americas between southern Georgia and Uruguay, and just about everywhere throughout the Gulf of Mexico and the Caribbean. There are numerous dive operators offering baited shark-diving virtually anywhere within this region, but the place where this kind of shark tourism started was in the Bahamas, notably on Grand Bahama and New Providence Island.

As we have discussed in other shark chapters, the whole 'baiting for shark tourism' issue is contentious, but if you want to see sharks in the water and you want to see them up-close and in their natural environment then they have to be baited. Probably the least intrusive way to bring the sharks to the divers is to put the remains of a fish inside a metal box with holes in it. The oils and scent released by the fish will cause the inquisitive reef sharks to come and investigate. Once they have approached it is unusual for them to leave until the box has been removed. The secret of trying to do this kind of dive as ethically as possible is to go with a reputable operator. The Caribbean Reef Shark is probably the most photographed and filmed shark species in the world, and as many of the Hollywood movies use the Caribbean as their backdrop, it is inevitably the one you will see most frequently on your screens if sharks are involved in the storyline. The reef sharks are members of the requiem shark family, which is part of the family Carcharhinidae and includes many of the migratory sharks, but the main feature is that their eyes are round and their pectoral fins sit entirely behind the five gill slits. The size of requiem sharks varies across the family, and some of them are at home in brackish or fresh water, while others can only tolerate seawater. It is unknown where the word requiem comes from, but the most likely option is that it comes from the Latin word meaning 'rest', a reference to their ability to stop moving, unlike most shark species.

OPPOSITE *A duo of reef sharks cruise over the coral reef.*

ABOVE *You can do a shark-feed dive where the guides wear chainmail and feed that sharks as they swim past.*

One of the key identification features of the reef shark is an extra rear tip on the second dorsal fin, and also the gill slits are longer, relatively, than most other species. Its colouration is also slightly unusual in that it has a copper-brown to dark grey upper surface and the lower, ventral side is usually more yellow than white. This species has the classic shark shape, with the slightly angled dorsal fin and long caudal or tail fin. Its snout, however, is more rounded and shorter than some sharks, giving it a particularly robust look. In addition to these features, it does have large eyes, and these enable them to hunt at depths of up to 400m (1,300ft) where the light is in short supply, although they are normally found on the edges of reefs or cruising across the reef in the shallow waters of continental shelves. They can grow up to 3m (10ft) long and weigh as much as 70kg (155lb) and many of the sharks of Providence are in this ballpark. The species has a reputation as a ferocious and efficient predator, but there are very few reports of attacks on humans, particularly divers.

The Caribbean Reef Shark, as its name suggests, favours the shorelines and reefs of the Caribbean. Their diet typically includes bony fish, cephalapods and crustaceans, although stingrays and eagle rays have been recorded as being taken regularly. Many observers believe that these elasmobranch cousins are their favourite prey.

The Caribbean Reef Shark is known to many divers and very few have ever felt threatened by their presence. The usual sightings are at a distance, as they tend to avoid interactions with humans, probably seeing us as a threat and therefore preferring to avoid us. No predator wants to become damaged in a fight, as this will reduce their fitness and their chances of survival. If they do feel threatened, their behaviour changes and they become obviously aggressive. They will swim in a zigzag motion and dip their pectoral fins every few seconds; this is normally the cue to move away gently. Since shark records began in 1960, there have been less than 30 documented attacks on humans by this species, of which not one was fatal and several were provoked. While the 'reefie' will turn up in great numbers if they have been baited, once the bait is taken away they will revert to their normal behaviour and go back to hunting on their own.

LEFT ABOVE *The bait can attract up to 20 sharks at any given time.*

LEFT BELOW *A Caribbean Reef Shark swims past a wreck in the clear blue water of the Bahamas.*

ABOVE *A bait box hidden on the reef will bring in plenty of sharks.*

OPPOSITE ABOVE *Caribbean Reef Sharks are sleek and elegant and one of the most beautiful sharks in the ocean.*

OPPOSITE BOTTOM *On the reef you will encounter sharks and get the chance to photograph them too.*

Like other requiem sharks, the Caribbean Reef Shark is viviparous, giving birth to between four and six live pups every other year. It is believed that the females migrate to the shallow waters of the north-western Brazilian coast to give birth and the young reef sharks stay in the shallow waters of this region until they grow large enough to be able to fend for themselves. The birth usually takes place in spring or late autumn.

Diving with any shark is a privilege and both of us have dived with several operators throughout the

Bahama chain who use the 'fish in a box' method of baiting them. For me, the best of all these dives was with Stuart Coves who put the box inside the wreck of a 25m (80ft) fishing boat. Within a short space of time there must have been 12–18 fully-grown Caribbean Reef Sharks cruising around the wreck in that laconic manner that is so typical of this particular species. We stayed on this wreck for over an hour and whether you have a camera or not, just watching these robust yet graceful sharks as they all cruise in the same direction around the ship and through the

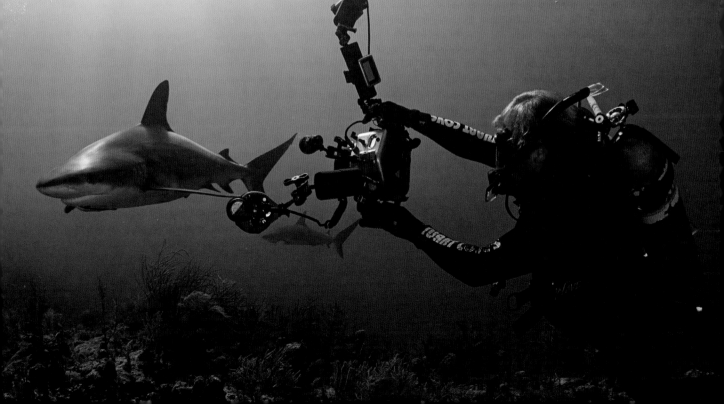

New Providence Island
BAHAMAS

KEY SPECIES
Caribbean Reef Shark (*Carcharhinus perezi*).

BEST TIME TO VISIT
The Bahamas offers diving with warm clear waters throughout the year. It might be best to avoid the peak hurricane season in September, but these islands are rarely affected severely.

TIPS FOR VISITORS
Give yourself plenty of time here as you are going to want to take in a variety of different dives, including several shark dives. Avoid the very busy holiday periods in the USA, including spring break, so that you have less-crowded diving and less-expensive accommodation.

EQUIPMENT TO TAKE
Ensure that you have an underwater camera/video with you along with plenty of memory cards. A thin wetsuit is all you will need for most of the year, but you might want a 3mm or 5mm wetsuit in the winter months.

ALTERNATIVE TOP DIVE SITES
You can find the Caribbean Reef Shark around many islands in this region and Jardines de la Reina off Cuba is another top dive site to see them.

windows and doorways is a wonderful experience. Another of the dives on offer, which is a bit more of a circus, is where one of the crew wear full chainmail, take a box of sliced-up fish pieces and use a long metal stick with a piece of fish on the end to bring the sharks in really close. Personally, I feel that this is taking the shark diving experience too far, but you certainly get to see them up close and personal, and the sharks are not afraid to bump and bash you as they squabble to be the first one to grab the fish. I don't believe anyone has ever been seriously hurt during this spectacle, but it has to be changing the behaviour of the shark in order to simply entertain the divers. Some will argue that this great experience will lead the divers to go away espousing how magnificent the sharks are, and changing people's opinions in a good way. However, if someone does get badly hurt the reputation of the shark will be far more damaged.

BELOW *A single shark swims over the head of a diver. These sharks are unfazed by the many divers that come to see them.*

The Hammerheads of Bimini

Being under the water with hammerheads is an incredible experience.
Given the fact that they really do look like they have been designed
by a committee of science fiction artists, you could be forgiven for
thinking that the whole dive was somewhat surreal.

The dive site at Bimini is a large expanse of soft white sand, and if you choose to do this shark dive you must be prepared for the fact that the operators will use fish as bait and will feed the sharks small pieces of fish in order to keep them interested. We have selected Bimini as the best dive site for the Great Hammerhead sharks because between the months of December and April you are almost guaranteed to see them. As stated, there are shark-diving operators who use bait to bring them in, and this will give you a close-up and personal experience with these amazing creatures that almost look like an extra from a Star Wars movie. There are some people who object to the use of bait to bring in sharks, but it is just a straightforward fact that if you want to see sharks, then you need to put down bait. This particular argument has been raging for as long as I can remember, and in all that time no permanent behavioural change has been seen in shark populations. It makes a lot of sense to do some research on the shark operator that you are likely to use and make sure you choose a responsible and professional outfit. In addition, the public's perception of sharks is slowly being improved and the use of shark-baiting is one of the reasons why.

There are other places to see these magnificent creatures apart from Bimini, and Great Hammerheads can be found in tropical waters to about 40° north and south of the equator. Like several other species of shark, Great Hammerheads may be found in waters less than 1m (3.3ft) deep and are actually known to acquire a suntan under these circumstances. Also, while they favour coral reefs, they are migratory animals and can be found virtually anywhere in this band of tropical and subtropical waters, often offshore at great depths.

There are 10 species of hammerhead shark in total. All are members of the Sphyrnidae family and each one has a familiar and distinctive hammerhead-shape.

OPPOSITE *One of the guides stands at the back to keep an eye on the sharks that go behind the diving group.*

This unusual structure, which is called a cephalofoil, contains several sensory organs, all of which are ultimately used for prey detection. This extended aquafoil distributes these receptors over a wider area and hence allows them to search for prey far more effectively than other sharks, despite the fact that all sharks have the sensory receptors, which are called ampullae of Lorenzini. Also, as a result of this unusual hammer-like head-shape, the eyes have evolved to be mounted on the ends of these extensions and this allows them to see 180° in a vertical plane on both sides of the body and therefore its horizontal vision is also greater than that of other sharks. However, they do have a small blind spot directly in front of the cephalofoil. One of the great features of the hammerhead shark is its ability to turn 360° within its own body length and in a vertical manoeuvre the cephalofoil is believed to assist in this, with the shark using it like the canard of an aircraft-wing.

Not only is the Great Hammerhead known for its agility, it has regularly been recorded at speeds in excess of 40km/h (25mph). While photographing these amazing creatures on a dive in Bimini, they would approach really slowly and then would turn around, directly in front of us, so as not to venture too far away from the bait box. Apart from the size, the cephalofoil is the principal means to distinguish the Great Hammerhead from the other species.

LEFT ABOVE *As well as high adrenalin shark dives, the Bahamas offers the perfect spots to unwind.*

LEFT BELOW *This is one of the best shark photography dives you can go on as it is in shallow and clear blue water.*

OPPOSITE *These usually shy sharks are tempted in by the smell of food and will come very close to divers and cameras.*

The great hammerhead shark swims just above the sand or just above the divers heads.
This species has evolved to have a huge sensory area between its eyes, giving it a very distinctive head-shape.
Their teeth-filled mouths are designed to catch prey on the seabed.

This feature on the Great Hammerhead is wider than on any of the others, typically about 25 per cent of its body length. It is also much straighter along the front than it is on any of its relatives. Another distinctive feature is its tall, sickle-shaped front dorsal fin, and while these differences may appear small, when looking at them alongside other species, the distinctions are really quite apparent.

The Great Hammerhead is the largest of all the hammerhead species, with full-grown females known to reach lengths of 5–6m (16–19.7ft) and weigh up to 450kg (1,000lb). The largest hammerhead ever recorded was a female, which measured 6.1m (20ft). Like most shark species, the males are generally much smaller, and full-grown male hammerheads tend to grow to around 3.5–4m (11.5–12ft). All species of hammerheads are viviparous, giving birth to live pups, and the Great Hammerhead has been known to produce litters of up to 55 young, although the average litter size varies between 12–40.

Hammerheads are not known to be aggressive towards divers, but there has been the occasional incident and like all wild animals, hammerheads should be respected. It is certainly respected by other reef sharks, and once fully grown the adults have no major predators on the reef. Juveniles, however, are susceptible to predation by larger sharks, particularly Bull Sharks (*Carcharhinus leucas*).

Bimini
BAHAMAS

KEY SPECIES
Great Hammerhead Shark (*Sphyrna mokarran*).

BEST TIME TO VISIT
Great Hammerheads are only in these waters
from December through to April.

TIPS FOR VISITORS
While the highlight of diving in Bimini is certainly the
hammerheads, there is plenty more to do, so stay a while
and see the dolphins, reefs and mangroves too.

EQUIPMENT TO TAKE
Ensure you have an underwater camera/video with you along
with plenty of memory cards. While the water is warm,
you spend this dive kneeling stationary on the seafloor, so
5mm suits, a hood and gloves are recommended.

ALTERNATIVE TOP DIVE SITES
While you can dive with other species of hammerhead shark
in many destinations, such as the Cocos Islands in Costa
Rica and Socorro in Mexico, Bimini is one of the few places
where you can get close to a Great Hammerhead Shark.

As a predator, the Great Hammerhead does not tend to specialize in prey. Its diet is known to include a large variety of invertebrates, many kinds of bony fish and even smaller sharks, including Grey Reef Sharks (*Carcharhinus amblyrhynchos*) and, occasionally, other hammerheads. Their preferred diet tends to be the cartilaginous fish – skates and rays – but they are known to be particularly fond of stingrays and in one specimen, which was caught off the coast of Florida, at least 96 stingray spines were found to be embedded in and around the mouth, and it is possible to assume that they are immune to the venom.

When hunting, the hammerheads use the sensors on the underside of the cephalofoil and sweep their heads across the seafloor looking to pick up the electrical signals given off by any stingrays that may be buried in the sand. It has also been known to take pelagic rays such as Spotted Eagle Rays (*Aetobatus narinari*), by taking a large bite from the ray's fin in order to disable it. Once the prey has been disabled, it is an easy task for the hammerhead to finish it off.

The Great Hammerhead is a magnificent animal, but it is in decline and is listed globally as an 'Endangered' species. This is mostly due to schools or individuals being caught up in fishing nets as bycatch. Along the western coast of Africa, the numbers have declined by an estimated 80 per cent in the last 25 years and the Great Hammerhead Shark is now listed as 'Critically Endangered'. Fishing in this region still continues to be unmonitored and unregulated and numbers are expected to decline even further unless action is taken to protect this most amazing shark.

BELOW *Some of the hammerheads can grow to over 5m (16ft) in length.*

Swimming Pigs
of The Exumas

When we were originally asked to compile this book, we inevitably
thought of all the obvious contenders which, hopefully, we have
included in one of the 32 chapters. However, while on a quest
to add to our portfolio of different wildlife dive sites around
the world, the thought of including swimming pigs had never
really crossed our minds.

We initially heard about them a few months after we started writing the book, from friends of ours who had recently come back from the Bahamas; we really had to go and see them.

When we show people our pictures of pigs as they swim in the classical, crystal-blue waters of the Bahamas, the first question that people ask us, once they are over their amazement, is: "how on earth did they get there?" We set about doing some research and came up with several conflicting theories. Like all hearsay and gossip, the facts have a tendency to become a little bit cloudy with time. The most likely story that we came across was by talking to the locals, and it dates back to over 20 years ago. Allegedly, it all started in 1992, when Iraq invaded Kuwait and

many people in the Bahama chain of islands were immediately concerned that the oil supply could very quickly dry up. Just like many people who live in island communities, fuel and oil for their transport and electricity needs is vital, and so a group of islanders decided to store a food source for what they anticipated to be a forthcoming supply shortage.

They gathered together a handful of pigs, which we believe are Gloucester Old Spots, and fenced them in on one of The Exuma's remote out-islands. Of course, for those who remember the conflict, it only lasted a few weeks and the disruption to the oil supply was minimal. The guys who had fenced in the pigs, apparently, forgot all about them and got on with their lives as before. Meanwhile, the pigs decided that they themselves

OPPOSITE *It is quite a sight to sit in the shallow water and have a pig walk right up to you.*

ABOVE *The beauty of The Exumas can clearly be seen as you take a small plane to fly in.*
OPPOSITE *The pigs look like they may once have been closely related to Gloucester Old Spots.*

needed food, broke out of their fencing and commenced foraging and truffling on the island. The island itself had very little food, especially for the likes of these full-grown pigs, but when they ventured down to the beach they discovered a plentiful supply. Sailing along the Bahamas chain is commonplace for many part-time and regular sailors, and as they were passing The Exumas, several of these sailors spotted these non-endemic creatures scurrying along the beach and pulled over to anchor and took a closer look. One can only imagine their thoughts as they saw these somewhat emaciated pigs wandering along the sand, but fortunately for the pigs, and the ensuing 'swimming pigs' tourists, they

decided to feed them with bread and fruit. It wasn't long before conversations and radio calls between sailing boats led to the knowledge, amongst this fraternity, of pigs on the island called Big Major Cay. No one is exactly sure when they started swimming out to the boats to get their food, but it has now become a daily ritual and there are even regular tourist trips from Great Exuma that take people to see the 'swimming pigs.'

There are several ways to reach the site. The most expensive is to hire or buy a sailing boat and head along the Bahama chain until you get to Exuma. The easiest way, however, is to book a day-trip

ABOVE *Now a famous tourist attraction, these pigs are well used to passing boats and will swim alongside in order to get food.*

OPPOSITE TOP *The pigs are fed treats from tourists and leftovers from passing yachts that moor here for an evening.*

OPPOSITE BOTTOM *There is very little natural shelter or food for these pigs on the small key where they live.*

with one of the several outfits who run up and down the chain, pointing out the highlights of the islands to the tourists. On these trips, the guides will slow down as they go past the islands that are owned by various celebrities. Some of these island homes look really welcoming and can actually be hired, at a ridiculously exorbitant rate, for parties or holidays. Others are fenced and guarded in a way commensurate with Stalag Luft 17 or some other prison camp. The guards and fencing at these locations, however, are designed to keep people out. A third option is to charter the speedboat yourself which, if there are a few of you, is probably worth doing as you could cut out all the celebrity worship and head straight to the pigs, spending the extra time photographing and enjoying them.

There are also other highlights along the way, such as the Bond cavern, which is very close to Norman's Cay. It was here that scenes from *Thunderball* and *Never Say Never Again* were filmed. The light shards inside these caverns can make for some incredible photo opportunities, while the waters hold some amazing sea life. Norman's Cay itself has an interesting, although somewhat sinister, recent past. In 1978, the drug baron Carlos Lehder arrived in Norman's Cay and very soon started purchasing large pieces of property on the island, including a home for himself, a hotel and an airstrip. He then began pushing everyone else off Norman's Cay and within a short space of time he had gained full control of the island. Before long, suspicious air traffic over the small island began to increase and armed guards could be seen

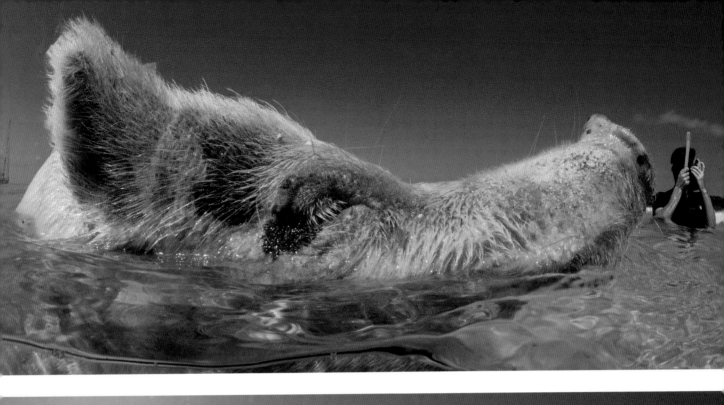

The Exumas
BAHAMAS

KEY SPECIES
Domestic Pig (*Sus domesticus*).

BEST TIME TO VISIT
The swimming pigs can be visited all year round.

TIPS FOR VISITORS
It is usually a full day trip out on the boat to reach Big Major Cay. Make the most of the whole experience and dive into the water at any of the stops to cool down and see what these tiny islands have to offer.

EQUIPMENT TO TAKE
You will be in the sun for most of the day, so have sunscreen, hats and rash vests with you. Take some healthy food for the pigs (apples are good) to give them a bit of variation from the usual bread rations.

ALTERNATIVE TOP DIVE SITES
The Exumas are surely the only place where pigs can be seen swimming in clear blue waters alongside the tourists that visit them.

patrolling the beaches. In the early 1980s, a Curtis C-47, allegedly carrying cocaine, crashed on take-off from Lehder's runway and the wreckage is still there today, lying in 2–3m (6.5–10ft) of water.

Not too far away from Norman's Cay is Compass Cay Marina. This is a place where large numbers of really quite bulky Nurse Sharks (*Ginglymostoma cirratum*) swim around the jetty. The marina workers have been feeding them for several years (hence the bulk) and they have become so used to humans that, if you stand up in the water, they will swim around between your

feet. If the tide is in, the water will cover the jetty and the Nurse Sharks have been known to skim across the top of it, or just lie there as the owner feeds them. He has even given them all names, and while it makes for a great photo opportunity, it is all a bit bizarre.

We felt that the swimming pigs were worthy of entry in a guide to the world's best dive sites purely and simply for the novelty value. They are unique and if you have your dive gear as you sail or ride along the lower cays of the Exuma chain, there is so much else to see, including the Nurse Sharks and sea stars.

BELOW *A highlight of a trip along the Exumas is to stop and see the swimming pigs.*

The American
Crocodiles of Cuba

Crocodiles and alligators can be seen all over the world in many tropical and subtropical regions. However, these relics of the dinosaur age are mostly unpredictable and aggressive and getting into the water to photograph these amazing predators can be a somewhat hazardous operation.

The American Crocodile, however, is far less aggressive than many other species. It is unlikely to attack anything much bigger than a small dog. This, of course, does not mean that getting into the water with one of these animals is entirely safe and that no harm could possibly come to you. These crocodiles are predators, and like any animal that kills for food, a lack of respect and knowledge of their behaviour could easily lead to a very dangerous situation. When you are face-to-face with a 3m (10ft) long American Crocodile and the lens or dome port of your camera housing is all but touching the business end of these many-toothed creatures, you are very much aware that a crocodile is a carnivore.

This crocodile certainly is a prehistoric-looking creature which can be distinguished from its close relative, the American Alligator (*Alligator mississippiensis*), by the several differences. It has a longer and thinner snout, its colouration is lighter and, when the jaws are closed, two long teeth on its lower jaw overlap the upper jaw.

One hundred miles off the south-east coast of Cuba lies an archipelago called Jardines de la Reina which, translated from the Spanish, means 'Gardens of the Queen'. The small islets that make up this archipelago are mostly sandbanks with stands of mangroves, and living among these mangroves are a small number of American Crocodiles which feed upon the fish that use the mangrove roots as their nursery. A small number of floating barges and boats are used by divers and fishermen who make the six-hour trek from the mainland to be rewarded with spectacular underwater photography and great fishing opportunities.

OPPOSITE *If you move stealthily you can get very close to the crocodiles.*

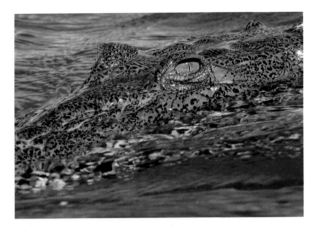

One of the crew of this operation is Gustavo Lopez Sanchez, a Cuban dive guide who has been working on the archipelago since 2008. During this time he has made contact with several of these magnificent reptiles and one in particular, called Nino, responds to his voice when he calls his name. It is an incredible sight when you venture out on a small skiff with Gustavo standing on the bow calling "Nino, Nino." The whole situation really is quite bizarre, and as you look around, you may be forgiven for thinking that this guy is crazy. However, more often than not, within a few minutes the croc's unmistakable snaking action can be seen moving towards us across the water with just his eyes and nostrils breaking the surface. Nino is just a baby at four years old, but at 3m (10ft) and with a huge array of really quite large and very white teeth, it is an amazing experience to slide into the water with a camera, protected by its underwater housing, and move to within inches of this magnificent apex predator. Nino allowed several of us to get in the water and get some 'up-close and personal' images, although we were careful to ensure that it was only one person at a time and that we were moving very gently with no jerky movements whatsoever.

American Crocodiles can be found along the Atlantic and Pacific coasts of southern Mexico to as far south as Peru and Venezuela. They inhabit many of the Caribbean islands and parts of the southern coast of the United States. It is one of the few crocodile species which tends to prefer the salinity of seawater to the freshwater of lakes and rivers. As a result, they are usually found in brackish lakes or mangrove swamps, such as those on the archipelago of Jardines de la Reina. The American Crocodile can also be found in coastal areas and they have

ABOVE TOP *Whilst the crocodiles here are wild, the chefs onboard some boats do feed them and they have become used to approaching vessels in order to obtain food.*

ABOVE BOTTOM *Two underwater photographers head out to see if they can get in the water with an American Crocodile.*

OPPOSITE *Their impressive teeth make them look ferocious, but the crocodiles prefer smaller prey and are unlikely to attack a diver.*

ABOVE *In very shallow water, this diver gets in close for a dentistry shot.*

OPPOSITE TOP *To see such a predator is the wild in clear still waters is a real privilege.*

OPPOSITE BOTTOM *The American Crocodiles found in Cuba often rest amongst the seagrass at the side of the mangroves.*

been known to move into river systems. They have become so well-adapted to living in saltwater that some populations can be found in hypersaline lakes.

Crocodiles are cold-blooded, or ectothermic, and therefore need a warm environment to be able to survive. They have to control their own temperature, keeping warm by lying in the sun and cooling off by sliding into the water. They are also known to use a process called 'gaping', which is where they lie with their mouths open to help keep them cool. It is very easy to understand that this action has been mistaken for aggressive behaviour

in the past, but it really is just one of several ways for the crocodiles to regulate their body temperature.

Nino is still quite small for a male American Crocodile as a full-grown male can be over 6m (20ft) long and weigh close to 1,000kg (2,200lb). Realistically, however, an average male, when fully grown, is more likely to be 4–5m (13–16.5ft) long and weigh around 400kg (880lb). Like all other crocodile species, the females are smaller and it is unusual for a female to exceed 4m (13ft).

Jardines de la Reina
CUBA

KEY SPECIES
American Crocodile (*Crocodylus acutus*).

BEST TIME TO VISIT
The prime time to dive here is between December and April, although the diving is excellent all year round. Avoid peak hurricane season between August and November.

TIPS FOR VISITORS
As the number of divers allowed to visit this marine park is limited, it is best to book well in advance. Ensure that you have enough time to include a stay in Havana. Do not expect phones or Wi-Fi to work well.

EQUIPMENT TO TAKE
Jardines de la Reina is only accessible via a liveaboard, so you need to make sure that you have everything you need before departure. Include plenty of spares, for example batteries. It is a long boat ride to a very remote site. A 5mm wetsuit is a good idea for long dives in water in which the temperature will be in the region of 25°C (77°F). For the shark-diving, it is best to have black gloves and boots.

ALTERNATIVE TOP DIVE SITES
Another great place to get in the water with American Crocodiles is Chinchorro Banks in Mexico.

Despite the large size of these reptiles, American Crocodiles rarely attack large animals and tend to feed on fish, small mammals, reptiles and birds. Attacks on humans by American Crocodiles are rare, which is reassuring for those getting close-up to Nino in the mangroves.

When you are there, you really are aware that this magnificent creature is a wild animal. What encourages you to be confident enough to get close to the crocodile is the knowledge that there is a special bond between Gustavo and Nino. Gustavo warned us before we went to find Nino, that if he was not comfortable that Nino was in the right frame of mind, then he would not have allowed us into the water.

The official IUCN Red List status of the American Crocodile is 'Vulnerable'. However, research is taking place and hopefully the information and increased awareness gained from any studies will help to improve its situation. The species has the most wide-ranging distribution of any New World crocodile, and in Cuba the populations are believed to be relatively healthy. This species is protected in most countries, but any protection can be difficult to enforce since it can be very difficult to tell one crocodile skin from another. In addition, the loss of the croc's habitat throughout this region is one of the main concerns for the future.

BELOW *A young crocodile swims over towards our boat.*

The Silky Sharks of Jardines de la Reina, Cuba

Although Silky Sharks can be seen in many locations around the world, I have chosen Jardines de la Reina as the pick of the bunch. The water throughout the archipelago is crystal clear nearly all year round. The whole area is a private marine park, where diver numbers are restricted to only 700 per year and this control of numbers and behaviour is almost certainly why the reef conditions and the wildlife are so pristine.

While the Silky Shark is considered to be one of the three most common pelagic sharks, along with the Oceanic Whitetip Shark (*Carcharhinus longimanus*) and the Blue Shark (*Prionace glauca*), the Silky is far more likely to be found in offshore waters where food is generally easier to come by. At this site the Silky Sharks can often be seen alongside Caribbean Reef Sharks (*Carcharhinus perezi*), and while their features are fairly similar, when you see them together you can appreciate the differences. The Silky Shark appears to be a far more intelligent, graceful and inquisitive creature.

These two species are certainly the most abundant sharks at this location, where the patchwork of small islands and mangroves provides the ideal nursery for all juvenile marine creatures. Sharks will be with you on every dive and they will be close to you. As a photographer, it can be very difficult to get a shot that doesn't have a photobombing Caribbean Reef Shark flashing through the middle of it. In addition to these two species you may also see Whitetip Reef Sharks (*Triaenodon obesus*), Lemon Sharks (*Negaprion brevirostris*) and possibly even hammerheads (genus *Sphyrna*). Whale Sharks (*Rhincodon typus*) are often seen between October and December and Nurse Sharks (*Ginglymostoma cirratum*) are a common sight at any time of the year. Despite these healthy numbers of large predators, and perhaps because of them, smaller marine life is abundant on the coral reefs, with the most vibrant and beautiful colours visible wherever you look.

OPPOSITE *A diver hangs just below the boat to get one last look at the sharks before returning to dry land.*

The Silky Sharks are slimmer and more streamlined than the reef sharks, with a long and rounded snout which is slightly more pointed than that of the reef shark, and they also have very fine flaps of skin in front of the nostrils. Their eyes, like a few other species of shark, are equipped with nictitating membranes, which act as a protective third eyelid.

Their pectoral fins are one of the main distinguishing features as they are narrow and falcate (sickle-shaped) and can become very long as they mature. The dorsal fin is relatively small, and they have a second dorsal fin, which is so small that it is sometimes difficult to spot. Like many species of shark they are bicoloured, with the upper half, or back, being a dark golden brown or possibly dark grey, while their underside is pure white. Silky Sharks usually reach a length of 2.5m (8ft), but can grow to 3.5m (11.5ft), with the female generally being larger than the male. In the Jardines de la Reina most of these amazing elasmobranchs were at least 2.5m (8ft) in length.

The Silky Shark feeds mainly on bony fish and cephalopods, and like their fellow requiem shark, the Blue Shark, they have been known to shepherd their prey into a large ball in order to be able to dart in open-mouthed and grab a meal. They have also been known to follow schools of tuna, which is one of their favourite prey items. The unfortunate side-effect of their affinity to tuna is that they are often taken as bycatch by tuna fishing vessels. The Silky Shark has excellent hearing and uses this finely tuned sense to home in on the noises generated by other animals that may be feeding or foraging. The Silky Shark is viviparous, which means that it gives birth to live young, in litters of around 10 to 15 pups. The young

ABOVE TOP *The sun sets over the liveaboard at the end of a great day of diving in Jardines de la Reina.*

ABOVE BOTTOM *The sharks will stay near the boat so long as there is the smell of dead fish in the water.*

ABOVE *The Silky Sharks swim in a fairly constant pattern around the bait box hanging at the back of the dive boat.*
OVERLEAF *Sometimes it is hard to leave the water and dives will last nearly two hours in the shallow water.*

sharks will spend several months developing their hunting skills in the mangroves and on the sheltered reef systems before they are large enough to venture out and face the dangers that lurk in the open ocean.

Fully grown Silky Sharks spend most of their time in the open ocean as pelagic predators and there have been occasional reports of them behaving aggressively towards divers. They have large cutting teeth and a bite from a Silky could be dangerous. However, the Silkies of Cuba are far more familiar and used to humans in the water and the dive guides who operate in this area claim that they have never been bitten or even felt threatened by a Silky Shark or a

reef shark. The Goliath Groupers and other larger groupers are far more likely to have a go at a diver if he or she has interfered with its food source.

Unfortunately, some of the latest data is now suggesting that Silky Shark numbers, like those of many other shark species, are declining around the world. With tuna being hunted virtually to extinction by humans, the Silky Sharks are getting caught up in the fishing nets. They are also specifically targeted for their fins before being thrown back into the ocean to die. This prompted the IUCN to reassess the conservation status for the Silky Shark in 2007 from 'Least Concern' to 'Near Threatened'.

Jardines de la Reina
CUBA

KEY SPECIES
Silky Shark (*Carcharhinus falciformis*).

BEST TIME TO VISIT
The prime time to dive here is between December and April,
although the diving is excellent all year round. Avoid peak
hurricane season between August and November.

TIPS FOR VISITORS
As the number of divers allowed to visit this marine park is limited, it is
best to book well in advance. Ensure that you have enough time to include
a stay in Havana. Do not expect phones or Wi-Fi to work well.

EQUIPMENT TO TAKE
Jardines de la Reina is only accessible via a liveaboard, so you need to make sure
that you have everything you need before departure. Include plenty of spares, for
example batteries. It is a long boat ride to a very remote site. A 5mm wetsuit is a
good idea for long dives in water in which the temperature will be in the region
of 25°C (77°F). For the shark-diving, it is best to have black gloves and boots.

ALTERNATIVE TOP DIVE SITES
Large schools of Silky Sharks are found around the Socorro Islands in
Mexico and divers regularly encounter them up-close in these waters.

Travelling to the Jardines de la Reina is not the easiest journey you're ever likely to make. You will almost certainly fly in to Havana, and from here it is a 6–7 hour road journey across the island to the small town of Jucaro. Jucaro is a small port and the journey across the straits to the archipelago takes another 5–6 hours on a small liveaboard called MV *Georgiana*. Because of the restrictions within the marine park, there really is only one way in which you can do this trip, and that is to stay on the liveaboard which brought you over to the archipelago in the first place. From here, the dive company which has the contract, 'Avalon', operates a dive skiff which ventures out three times a day to take you to one of the dive sites. According to the dive guides, who are all experienced, the Silky Sharks are here all year round and so, while the trip is quite expensive and the journey to get there is a long one, you are at least guaranteed to be able to dive with the Silky Sharks. It is not a distant interaction either. As long as you remain calm, hang in the water and do not try to pursue or harass them in order to get a closer look or image, they will come in really close to you. Most of the images in this chapter were taken with a fisheye lens, which gives you an idea of how close they were to the divers.

BELOW *If you familiarize yourself with the swimming pattern of a particular shark you can get close to these somewhat shy creatures.*

The Humpback Whales
of Grand Turk

Grand Turk, a part of the Turks and Caicos Islands, is a small island
at the southern end of the Bahama Islands chain or, if you prefer,
the northern end of the Caribbean. The main town, Cockburn, is
the capital of this British Overseas Territory, but it would be very
hard to describe it as a city.

The streets of Cockburn are lined with many original colonial buildings, but this is not a place to stand on ceremony as donkeys and wild horses stroll casually along the dusty roads. The people here are friendly and the atmosphere is relaxed to the extreme, even by Caribbean standards. The Turks and Caicos Islands are part of the same chain of islands that includes The Bahamas, yet these islands very much retain their own identity and atmosphere. They comprise eight islands and 41 small cays, of which only nine are inhabited, with Grand Turk sitting to the east of the Bahamas and the other Caicos islands. It is only 10km (6 miles) long and at its widest point is barely 3km (2 miles) across. The town of Cockburn has a rich history, with an initial economic industry of salt production using seawater ponds called salinas to evaporate seawater and retain the salt and minerals. The water enters the salinas through sluice gates, and while no longer functional, the gates and the salinas are still in evidence.

The island of Grand Turk is one of the many claimed first landfall sites of Christopher Columbus and it gained fame in the 1960s as the landing site of the NASA *Friendship 7* spacecraft. *Friendship 7* was the first spacecraft to orbit the earth and was piloted by John Glenn. Local folklore would have you believe that he saw the white sand beaches of Grand Turk from his orbit in space and decided that this would be the perfect place to land a space vehicle. In more recent times, however, it has been scuba diving and visiting cruise ships that have driven the local economy.

OPPOSITE *A spyhopping Humpback Whale takes a look at the dive boat.*

Gibbs Cay is a popular place to picnic and see stingrays and Lemon Sharks swimming in the shallow water.

The island is very small and is surrounded by perfect white sandy beaches and turquoise waters of various shades, depending on the depth. Just 100m (330ft) or so off the coastline on the Caribbean side of the island, the topography plummets into an abyss. The reef, which borders almost the entire length of the Caribbean side of the island, rises up from the sand for 5–10m (16.5–33ft) and it is here that the top of the abyss wall begins. Leading down to the abyss, the wall starts at a relatively shallow 10m (33ft), but then drops in a near-perfect vertical descent to over 2,000m (6,560ft). This abyss creates a passage that separates the Turks Islands from the Caicos

Islands and it is along this wall that Humpback Whales migrate during the early months of the year as they make their journey to the Silver Banks of the Dominican Republic. It is here that they give birth to a new generation of Humpbacks.

The Humpback Whale is a species of baleen whale that can grow up to 18m (60ft) in length and weigh in at over 40 tonnes. They are well known for their long pectoral fins, which can be up to 5m (16.5ft) in length, and these fins often become covered in barnacles and other freeloaders. The whale's scientific name, *Megaptera novaeangliae*, means 'big-winged

ABOVE *Humpback Whales migrate along the island chain on their way to the Silver Banks.*

New Englander' and it gets this name as a result of the fact that the New England whale population was the first one to be known to the Europeans exploring the New World. These long fins give them incredible manoeuvrability; they can be used to slow the whale down or even to move it backwards.

These leviathans are popular with whale-watchers from all over the world, as they are not shy in performing tail- and fin-slaps on the surface of the water and even regularly breach, throwing their huge bodies completely clear of the surface of the water. If you find yourself diving off the wall between the months of January and April, you would be very unlucky not to hear the haunting whale song as it travels through the water, and even if you do not get lucky and catch a glimpse, the song is truly magical.

The wall itself is covered in orange sponges, rare black gorgonians and classic Caribbean corals, and is teeming with marine life. One of the macro subjects that Grand Turk is famous for, is the Flamingo Tongue Snail (*Cyphoma gibbosum*). If you have a keen eye, or if you are following a guide who knows where to search, you can find these tiny snails feeding on soft corals. These marine molluscs convert toxins

ABOVE *Pristine reefs grow here and are at their best in years when there has been a long gap between hurricanes.*

ABOVE *Clear blue water contrasts with the yellow sponges that grow all around these reefs.*

from their food into toxic chemicals which protect them from predators. These toxins are deposited in the mantle, and the mantle also performs a similar function to the branchia of nudibranchs, absorbing oxygen and releasing carbon dioxide. The Flamingo Tongue Snail is a member of the family Ovulidae, all of which are also known as false cowries, and looking at the mantle it is quite easy to see why. Members of this family vary considerably in size, but they are all either predatory or parasitic.

Another creature which can regularly be seen meandering along shallow, sandy areas of the seabed is the conch (pronounced conk). This popular delicacy of Grand Turk (although it is illegal to export them) is served up at every local barbecue, either in the form of conch fritters, or fresh in the local delicacy: conch salad. Barracuda, grouper and hogfish make up the larger reef fish that populate the open areas alongside the wall and it is a common experience to see several species of shark, or a school

ABOVE *Bright tropical reef fish hug the corals on the side of the wall for safety.*

ABOVE *Whilst diving along the wall in Grand Turk you can hear the song of the Humpback Whale.*

of Spotted Eagle Rays (*Aetobatus narinari*), if you take the time to look out into the deep blue sea.

The dive site called 'The Tunnels' is a particular highlight as it offers divers of all levels a unique opportunity to make their way to the vertical reef wall. As the name suggests, you can fin your way through tubes of rock, covered in black corals and sponges, along the sandy seabed until you get to a long sandy shoot. This downward-sloping, divable

shoot will deposit you out into the deep blue water that butts up against the colourful reef wall. Several years ago there was a trend for divers to overweight themselves and 'ski' down the slope on their fins, before making a ski jump into the blue.

Another worthwhile trip which can be taken from Grand Turk visits the tiny uninhabited island called Gibbs Cay. This white-sanded gem is a popular destination to see the large Southern

Grand Turk
TURKS AND CAICOS ISLANDS

KEY SPECIES
Humpback Whale (*Megaptera novaeangliae*).

BEST TIME TO VISIT
If you want to see the Humpback Whales then the best time of year is between late January and early April. The general diving is great here all year round, but avoid August and September as these are the months most likely to be adversely affected by tropical storms.

TIPS FOR VISITORS
Grand Turk offers great diving and is also very close to the Bahamas, making it a great option for a dual-destination trip.

EQUIPMENT TO TAKE
A 3mm wetsuit is fine for the summer months and a 5mm is advised during winter. For whale-watching, have a camera on hand while on the boat, with a good long lens to get shots of breaching whales.

ALTERNATIVE TOP DIVE SITES
South Africa during the Sardine Run sees large numbers of Humpback Whales migrate up the coast. Tonga also offers great opportunities to get into the water with both adults and juveniles.

Stingrays (*Dasyatis americana*) that have made this place their home, along with the juvenile Lemon Sharks (*Negaprion brevirostris*), which have become accustomed to being fed snacks by visiting tourists. You can wade into the warm clear water and the stingrays will swim right up to you to check if you have any morsels of food for them. Be warned, however, that these magnificent animals have absolutely no concept of personal space, and if you are uncomfortable at being buffeted by a stingray which may have a wingspan of over 1m (3.3ft), then you may just prefer to watch. There are many other folk who just come here to have a conch barbecue on a perfect white beach on an uninhabited Caribbean island.

BELOW *Grand Turk is a quiet island and you will almost certainly get the reef to yourself.*

The Turtles of Statia

As is the case with many of the dive sites we've covered in this book,
if you really want to go and see something unusual and amazing
then often you have to get off the beaten track. A lot of these remote
locations are amazing because the reefs have not been damaged by
too many divers or other human activities.

Just to the south of the Bahamas chain lies another group of islands, generally referred to as the West Indies, and among the islands at the northern end of this chain are three which form part of the Netherlands Antilles; these are St. Martin, Saba and St. Eustatius. It is the least known of these islands, St. Eustatius, or Statia as it is more commonly known, where large numbers of Hawksbill Turtles congregate. This very small island has less than 1,500 permanent human residents and dimensions of approximately 5km (3 miles) by 1.6km (1 mile). Wrecks have been deliberately sunk as artificial reefs since the 1990s in order to attract diver tourism. There are also remnants of old wooden ships, some of which are over 300 years old, lying just off the west coast of this island. This serves as a reminder of a once-proud heyday when Statia was one of the biggest trading ports of the Caribbean. The wealth of this tiny island led to it being known as the Golden

Rock, as so many different nations were using it for trading. It also has its own special part in history, in that it was the first country to officially recognize the United States during their war of independence with the United Kingdom. They did this by firing a 30-gun salute as the US vessel, the brig of war, *Andrew Doria* entered the harbour. *Andrew Doria* replied with its own 11-gun salute in response to the island's recognition of the United States as a nation.

The diving on this little-known island is excellent as the reefs are in such great condition, largely due to the relatively small number of divers who make the effort to get here. There are very few pelagic creatures that come into the island reef system, but you would be unlucky not to see the occasional reef shark, and Spotted Eagle Rays (*Aetobatus narinari*) are not unusual either. It is, however, the wrecks that have been sunk to create artificial reefs that make Statia

OPPOSITE *Many of the turtles in St Eustatius have made their homes in the handful of deliberately-sunk wrecks around the island.*

266

such a special place to dive. The jewel in the crown
is the *Charles L Brown*, which was once the property
of Cable & Wireless. Having purchased a new and
modern cable-layer, the company did not want to
see this ship falling into the hands of a competitor
who would be able to undercut them on price, since
it was still serviceable. It is believed that this 100m
(330ft) long vessel laid the first fibre-optic cable
across the Atlantic Ocean from the United States
to Ireland. However, neither of us has actually been
able to find any proof of this and it is probably an
island myth. We do know that it did a lot of cable-
laying work around the Caribbean. The government
of Statia bought the ship on eBay for US$1 on the
understanding that it would be sunk as an artificial
reef. It is now a really impressive dive site with its hull
lying on its starboard side at a depth of 28m (92ft).

While the Hawksbills can be found on this wreck
during the day and the night, it is a more recently
sunk wreck called the *Chien Tong* that seems to attract
the largest numbers of them during the night. The
Chien Tong was once a fishing trawler, and having
worked with a research group from the University
of Swansea on a tagging programme, it appears that
while there may be 10 to 20 turtles sleeping here
overnight, very few of them are returnees and the
university project team is still looking for reasons why.
Most of the turtles are around 1m (3.3ft) or less but,
on night dives, enormous turtles nearly 2m (6.5ft)
long can be seen with their heads sticking into a
crevice, presumably in the belief that they are hidden.

The wreck of the *Chien Tong* is itself an impressive
dive site. It lies upright on its hull at a maximum
depth of 18m (60ft). There are numerous swim-

ABOVE *Turtles have to go to the surface to breathe and then dive
back down to the reef to continue feeding.*

OPPOSITE *A small Green Turtle tucks itself into the handrail of
the* Chien Tong *wreck for a snooze.*

throughs and as the wreck is only 60m (200ft) long, it is very easy to get all around the wreck and in and out of some of the swim-throughs on a single dive. I have dived this wreck numerous times and have never failed to see at least one turtle, normally a Hawksbill, but I have also seen several Green Turtles (*Chelonia mydas*).

This is a classic wreck-dive, but it is on a night dive that this wreck really comes to life as both resident and transiting turtles find somewhere to hide for their overnight stay. It appears that the whole wreck is covered in bright orange and red sponges, as you flash your dive light across the metal structure these colours just fill your vision. It won't be long before you come across several of the sea dwelling chelonians either swimming across your vision or hiding in one of the many nooks and crannies on the wreck. On a good night, if you are looking, you may see as many as 10–15 turtles and considering the Hawksbill Turtle is listed as Critically Endangered, it really is a truly incredible experience. As I mentioned earlier, you may see a Green Turtle, and while this species is not in quite the same trouble as the Hawksbill it is still designated as 'Endangered' both in the USA and internationally. It is the shells of these wonderful underwater reptiles that make them so attractive to the immoral and uncaring poachers, but fortunately for the turtles they are well protected throughout the Caribbean. It is probably the protection afforded to them in this region that helps to account for their prolific numbers on this island.

On the eastern side of the island there is a sandy beach that is about 3.2km (2 miles) long, and it is here that the female Hawksbills come to lay their eggs. Statia has its own marine and National Park organisation known

ABOVE *The largest of the artificial reefs on Statia is a wreck called the* Charles L Brown, *which is also known as 'the Charlie Brown'.*

ABOVE *The best time to see turtles on Statia is on a night dive when they come to the wrecks to sleep.*

as STENAPA, which is a not-for-profit organisation that relies on volunteers, mostly gap-year students from the US, UK and the Netherlands. The turtles and their eggs are fiercely protected and even driving a vehicle along the beach is banned to prevent the eggs from being inadvertently damaged. STENAPA also looks after the island's environment. It has a volcano at either end of the island, one of which is extinct, and the other dormant. The dormant volcano is called the Quill and

inside this volcano is a Caribbean rainforest with its own ecosystem. We lived on this volcano for over a year and every now and again we would feel her rumble. It lies on the same fault line as Montserrat and so it is unlikely to erupt as Montserrat would blow first.

If you ever decide that you would like to dive the island of St. Eustatius, it is a very different experience from any you are likely to have encountered elsewhere.

St Eustatius

KEY SPECIES
Hawksbill Turtle (*Eretmochelys imbricata*).

BEST TIME TO VISIT
St Eustatius is a year-round dive destination, although you may want to avoid August and September due to the increased chance of tropical storms. The turtles are there all year round, but in addition to seeing them underwater, from April to October they nest on the island's beaches.

TIPS FOR VISITORS
St Eustatius is a quiet island, so do not expect to be out partying every night of the week here. Do take some time to walk up the island's dormant volcano (The Quill) and to see some of the land-based local wildlife. Also make sure you do a night dive on one of the artificial reefs to see large numbers of the turtles sleeping.

EQUIPMENT TO TAKE
The water is consistently pleasant so a 3mm wetsuit is fine for people who are not susceptible to the cold.

ALTERNATIVE TOP DIVE SITES
Tenerife in the Canary Islands and Sipadan in Malaysia are two great alternatives where you can see plenty of turtles on your dives.

The island is friendly, the islanders all speak English as a first language, and much of the remains of the island's history still exists. There is virtually no crime on the island, and when you step off the island-hopper you can almost believe that you have stepped back 20 or 30 years, and any stress you may have brought with you will be very quickly carried away by the gentle trade winds that caress this special island.

BELOW *The turtles seem undisturbed by the handful of divers that come to any given site during the day.*

The Whale Sharks
of Isla Mujeres

Isla Mujeres is a thin strip of land about 7km (4 miles) long which lies
in the Caribbean Sea around 7km (4 miles) off the Yucatán Peninsula
of Mexico. It was a sacred place to the Maya people and when the
Spanish arrived they found many images of goddesses, which in turn
gave this island its name, which translates as 'Island of Women'.

The island boasts beautiful white beaches, palm trees and clear water that changes from bright turquoise lapping against the sand to deep azure as the water deepens offshore. Many tourists come here to dive, relax and see the local wildlife, but there is one event that happens here each year that has made this tiny island a true wildlife-watching destination; the Whale Sharks.

It was local fishermen who first discovered that in the summer months, between June and September, large numbers of Whale Sharks would visit the waters just north of the island. This is a time when bonito fish are spawning, releasing huge numbers of eggs into the water, resulting in a bonanza food-fest for the filter-feeding Whale Shark. Once word got around that hundreds of Whale Sharks were gathering here to feed, in such a small area, tourism based around snorkelling with these gentle giants boomed. Now it is not just the Whale Sharks that flock here in the summer months, but the tourists too, all wanting to experience being in the water with the biggest fish in the sea.

The Whale Shark is the largest of all fish and individuals have been known to reach over 12m (40ft) in length and to weigh in at over 21 tonnes. They feed by swimming slowly with their huge mouths open, allowing water to rush past its filter pads, which remove any plankton, small fish, squid or eggs. They can also feed while stationary by opening and shutting their giant mouths, which creates a vacuum that sucks in large volumes of water.

OPPOSITE *Their patterns of spots can be used by scientists to individually identify sharks that visit these waters.*

Isla Mujeres holds the record for the largest ever Whale Shark aggregation, with over 400 individuals counted on a single day. Like human fingerprints, Whale Sharks each have a unique pattern of spots which allows them to be identified. Many marine charities and research organisations are now using photos taken by tourists to catalogue all the individuals that arrive at feeding grounds such as Isla Mujeres, so do be sure to investigate whether you can assist with their conservation efforts by donating your images.

While the Whale Shark is listed as 'Vulnerable' on the IUCN's Red List, it is still hunted for its fins and meat, and also suffers casualties from boat strikes and entanglement in fishing nets. Very little is known about their movements and breeding cycles, but the aggregation of Whale Sharks in Isla Mujeres has allowed scientists to tag many individuals in one place and to learn about their migration and feeding patterns. Unfortunately, we are still a very long way from effectively protecting them.

With Whale Shark spotting becoming so popular in this area, as many as 100 boats may leave each morning to try and find the particular area where these giants are feeding. It may take several hours of patrolling the surface to find them, but once they have been found it will not only be Whale Sharks in large numbers,

LEFT TOP *The Whale Shark opens its huge mouth to take in as much food as possible.*

LEFT BOTTOM *Their food of plankton and fish eggs are often floating near the surface.*

OPPOSITE *Sometimes the sharks will swim up to the surface vertically so you need to watch all around you when you are in the water.*

ABOVE *Whale Sharks gather here in large numbers and swim close to the surface looking for food.*

but tourists too. The government, along with local scientists, have come up with strict guidelines to try and protect the sharks from too much intrusion. Any tours outside the official season (the dates of which are announced each year) are strictly prohibited. Each boat will have a limit on how many people it can take, and everyone must stay at the surface with no scuba diving allowed. Underwater photographers may not use flash photography – this measure was introduced to try and reduce disturbance to the sharks' feeding. Tourists must use biodegradable sunblock and may not touch the Whale Sharks at any time. On some days it can be too rough for the boats to head out, giving the Whale Sharks a break from the excessive numbers of people in the water. The standard tourist boat will take you out and you will take it in turns to get in the water until it is time to head back, with only two guests and the guide being allowed in the water at any time. A far better experience is to go with a dedicated photography boat, which will head out earlier than most of the standard tourist boats and will also stay out longer, giving you the beginning and end of the day without the crowds. These trips will spend several days on the water, giving you much more time to see these majestic creatures.

While Whale Sharks can be described as slow-moving filter-feeding sharks, with their average speed estimated at around 5km/h (3mph), trying

The sharks can swim much faster than any diver and it is vital that these animals are disturbed as little as possible.

to keep up with one swimming is impossible for any length of time. It is far better to spend some time watching their feeding pattern and then to get in the water where you think they will swim past and just stay still and watch. There can be so many sharks in the water, that you can simply float in one place and trust that they will approach you.

While out in the open sea, perhaps waiting for the next wave of Whale Sharks to swim past, keep your eyes open, as there are other creatures that come to feed here which are well worth the visit. Huge manta rays visit this site to feed at the same time as the Whale Sharks and you might also see sailfish, tuna and other open-sea

marine life. During this period, the bonito spawning can be so intense, that the water becomes cloudy with their eggs, but most of the time the water here is clear and the visibility good, making it a world class site for marine life encounters, particularly for photographers.

Isla Mujeres offers a jaw-dropping experience that is relatively easy to organize. Just being in the water with these giants is an experience that you will never forget. Each is the size of a double-decker bus and there can be hundreds of them feeding near the surface as you swim with them. Their mouths are over 1m (3.3ft) wide, and you need to be careful to avoid both their large gaping mouths and their powerful tails as they

Isla Mujeres
MEXICO

KEY SPECIES
Whale Shark (*Rhincodon typus*).

BEST TIME TO VISIT
Strict dates are set each year for the Whale Shark encounters,
usually between the beginning of June and September.

TIPS FOR VISITORS
Weather and wild animals can never be 100 per cent guaranteed,
so ensure that you have a few days booked on Isla Mujeres to
increase the likelihood of a good Whale Shark encounter.

EQUIPMENT TO TAKE
While the water is a warm 28–30°C (82–86°F), bring a full 3mm wetsuit, which
will stop you from burning while spending the day on the boat and at the surface
of the water. You do not need your dive kit, so travel light. Photographers can also
leave their strobes behind as flash photography in the water is not permitted.

ALTERNATIVE TOP DIVE SITES
Ningaloo Reef in Western Australia, Djibouti and Tofo Beach
in Mozambique are great places to see these magnificent
sharks, but there are plenty of other destinations too.

sweep through the water gathering huge quantities of the tiny food particles which they eat. With eyes widely positioned on each side of the head, they may not see you in their blind spot if you are directly in front, so it is up to you to move out of their way. They certainly do not seem to be bothered by the snorkelers in the water and carry on their continuous feeding frenzy regardless of all the people that have come to see them.

With flat calm seas, on a sunny day, in clear blue warm water, watching one of the most spectacular animal gathering events is awe-inspiring. Being on the surface of the water while the biggest fish in the ocean swims past you, mouth open wide to take in as much food as possible, has to be right up there with the best of all animal encounters. Isla Mujeres is a place that offers one of the best marine life encounter experiences in the world.

BELOW *Whale Sharks will pass very close to the snorkelers and so there is no need to chase them and scare them away.*
OVERLEAF *Scuba diving is not allowed with the Whale Sharks at Isla Mujeres so you will be snorkeling and freediving.*

Acknowledgements

All images in this book are by Nick and Caroline Robertson-Brown of Frogfish Photography except for the ones listed as follows:

All underwater images in the chapter about the Great White Sharks of the Neptune Islands were kindly donated by Andrew Fox (www.rodneyfox.com.au).

All images in the chapter about the Whale Sharks of Isla Mujeres were kindly donated by Daniel Norwood (www.danielnorwoodphotography.com).

Two of the images in the chapter about the manta rays of the Maldives were kindly donated by Sean Chinn (www.facebook.com/greatwhitesean).

All the images in the chapter about the Devil Rays of the Azores were kindly donated by Liz and Dave Skinner (www.skindivers.uk)

All the images in the chapter about the Short-tailed Stingrays of the Poor Knights Islands were kindly donated by Alex Misiewicz (www.bluzone.com)

The images about the SS *Yongala* were sourced from Tourism and Events Queensland (www.teq.queensland.com).

We have accumulated a large number of images from our diving trips of the wildlife and dive sites over the years, and many of these have been included in the book. There were, however, many more places that we needed to visit in order to cover the 32 dive sites that we wanted to portray as 'the best'. A number of people and organizations assisted us in getting the images, and visiting the sites that we really wanted to add; they are:

Bahamas Tourist Board
Rodney Fox Shark Expeditions
South Australia Tourist Board
Emperor Divers and Diverse Travel
The Scuba Place
Mares
Steve Warren from INON UK

In addition, we would like to say a very special thank you to Nick Barrett for his tireless proof-reading and painstaking attention to detail.

Index